REFLECTED

REFLECTED LIGHT

Responses to the creative arts

Edited by Joy Howard

GREY HEN

First published in 2020 by Grey Hen Press
PO Box 269
Kendal
Cumbria
LA9 9FE
www.greyhenpress.com

ISBN 978-1-9996903-6-6
Collection Copyright © Joy Howard 2020

Printed by Flexpress, Birstall, Leicester LE4 3BY

i. m. Barbara Burford

(1944 - 2010)

There are two ways of spreading light: to be the candle or the mirror that reflects it.

Edith Wharton

Preface

The idea for this book came from a group of poems that were submitted for the recent Grey Hen anthology of 'found' poems, *Out of Context*, but didn't quite fit. What they shared was a sense of paying homage to, and being inspired by, the work of other poets. I am aware of a huge level of interest in ekphrastic poetry at present – by definition poetic interpretations of paintings and graphic art. I felt there might be scope to extend this concept, and have a look at responses to other forms of creative arts. I already had the evidence in the case of poets on poetry. Widening the brief as far as possible, I received poems on sculpture, music, film and photography, museums and galleries, architecture, artefacts, exhibitions and installations as well as poetry. And of course paintings. Inevitably perhaps, because it has become an established form, these submissions outnumbered those on other art forms, and made selecting from them an especially difficult task. But here is a cornucopia of fascinating, intriguing and celebratory poetry on everything from the sublimity of cathedrals to the homely art of table setting.

The process of collecting these poems has been immensely rewarding. Google has been put hard to work and I have acquired a wealth of new knowledge and found much to delight and surprise. Each of the themed sections within is worthy of a book in itself – and there is enough here I hope to inspire someone else to produce one.

Joy Howard

Contents

the pulse of us

wearing an alternative skin

that we make such things

source of the blaze

Foreword

This is one of the most satisfying anthologies I've read for years. Grey Hen publications always offer a lot to the reader, and *Reflected Light* is no exception: strong and characteristically original. We're familiar with poems inspired by paintings, but this collection is richer, responding as it does to the freedom of a far wider range of forms of creativity, areas seldom or never examined before in quite this way. As one form of creative art responds to another, we have here poetry that attends to everything from environmental catastrophe to pottery designs, from knitting to cathedrals, from world famous paintings to graffiti, and which includes artefacts, exhibitions and installations of all sorts.

Each of these poets has her own tried and experienced voice; you are among skilful friends and the conversation's easy: there is comedy, sympathy, passion; there's a lot of warmth, a lot of affection, and as you read, you're oddly aware of *learning* so much along the way.

I read *Reflected Light* in one go, and at the end found myself unexpectedly excited, refreshed, as though my mind had just come out of the sea, clean, stimulated and energized. It opens the windows of the mind, as well as the eye. It's an anthology to treasure: an absolute delight.

R V Bailey

to leap between worlds

Everybody looks below the surface hoping they'll find some
meaning, some remnant of a wreck, cargo of lost gold, if they just
look hard enough and deep, when all they need is a glance. It's
enough to brush the surface lightly with a gaze, here, where a fish
can jump through air or a bird dive under water, where light breaks
and joins itself.

Imagine gazing at the green surface of the water. Your face, the
trees, mountains and sky are there. One sigh of the wind is all it
takes and everything's gone, face, trees, stone, clouds and you have
to wait till it comes back the same way you wait for your pleasure,
slippery as a fish, to leap between worlds out of the water, through
air, and back again.

Maria Jastrezębska

lifted out of time

Arrangement in Grey and Black No 1

After he'd finished the painting he gave it that title.
Critics had other words:
A painting of convalescence, said one.
An infinite fineness of greys, said another.
And a third found it, *Drearily smoky*
and wished Mr Whistler, *would stop using his palette*
of mud and clay and paint again like a gentleman.

She'd only sat for him
when the model failed to arrive
there, at the house in Chelsea.
In her widow's black and her cap
she sits with her feet on a stool,
the skirt of her dress tented about her.
And her hands, that could be arthritic,
rest in a froth of white lace on her lap.
Her face has the look of a mother
who wonders, how that small boy,
who required her right from the start
to be at his bidding,
is so much in charge of her now.

She'd seen portraits, knows
the youthful white beauties,
the languor, the lilies, the fine silks of society.
She stares ahead, not quite resigned,
her loneliness stranded against the wall.
Her dress edges are almost transparent
and her look is distant, lifted out of her time.

In another life she'll go on tour –
pull the crowds round Depressed America.
Her painted uprightness, her motherly presence
will comfort the nation, be engraved
on its stamps. As she looks ahead
does she see Edward Hopper's lonely people
framed alone but in late-night neon.

Josie Walsh

J M Whistler: *Portrait of the Artist's Mother*

What Do You See?

My blunt features, my small dark eyes?
I see red flaring

over cheek, nose and chin, I see green
crowding the red, shadowing
the face, I see my long blue

self, swaddled, an apron tied
in a half bow at the waist. But the hands,
the resting hands, how they

bring highlights into the lap
and on the right hand a scar of light
from wrist to knuckle!

And what of this cup,
round and balanced
in the saucer? The coffee pot glints

and the red tablecloth
tugs at my throat.

Nora Hughes

Paul Cézanne: *Woman with a Coffee Pot*

Interior

A young boy in a black woollen hat
looks at me as if I've said *no*
to going out to play. This afternoon
he must stay inside, sit still as held air
while his family work on
and the painter eases snow-light
over the low room. I imagine a tiled
enamel stove burning in a corner to keep
spinning and knitting hands moving
take the chill off the brushed wooden floor.
To the left a young woman in a vermilion scarf
stops to pare fruit, a dog begs at the feet
of little Suzanne, and every wall glows
in trompe-l'oeil – biblical and bright.
By the window beyond burnt-orange rugs
folded over old knees, two rifles hang
the way I might place a mirror
or a bowl of lilies.

Kerry Darbishire

Carl Larsson: *The Winter Cottage*

The Presentation

She owns the bottom half of the painting, so near and
present that Longhi must be in her small enclosure,
his feet scuffing wisps of hay that fell from her mouth,
his nostrils clenched against her faecal odour.

Freak remnant of an antediluvian era,
her black bulk gross, unendearing, Clara
eclipses the glittered noblewoman
the spectacle seems to be for.

Out of an arc of three masked protectors
the lady regards the beast or the artist or us
unenchanted. The showman lofts a whip
and a horn, which may mean nothing

but this is Carnival Venice and anything goes
including the mute despair of a captive rhinoceros.

Frances Nagle

Pietro Longhi: *Exhibition of a Rhinoceros*

Eve Speaks

This is *his* dream, mind.
This hothouse gloom,
the fleshy lotus flowers,
his darling shock-eyed lions
blundering through the bushes.
Would I have chosen
to lounge naked on one hip
purely for his delectation,
with his foliage reaching out
to finger me? To affect
this studio pose, drawing-room
smile, while pretending
to be so pleased with life?
Frozen for eternity
in someone else's dream.
Adam's. Henri's. Even God's.
Take your pick. (You'll see
that none of them are here.)
Let the charmer fumble
his notes. I'm all ears. Ready
for a bite of that forbidden fruit,
dozens of whose golden orbs
are dangling overhead.
Just let me out of Eden.
Give me a windy headland,
the vanilla scent of gorse
and adders basking
among the bracken,
some earnest little ship
beating her way southwards
through the waves, just a smudge
on the far horizon.

Ruth Sharman

Henri Rousseau: *The Dream*

25

Brush Stroke

Here, everything you see is doubled: two worlds
stand looking at one another, unable to see

the other. Out of reach and on a brink.
The eye of water fills with tree tears,

blinks, but won't hide what's there to see.
Imagine cupping water in your palms

and as you bend your neck to sip you catch
the moon of your face. 'Drink', it says,

so you drink in sky, passing clouds,
light gathered in shadows of the wood;

feel them slide down your throat as you swallow,
putting down roots, throwing high their branches

with leaves like notes in a score. Whatever else
it might do, water can't not tell truth.

Rebecca Gethin

David Milne: *Bishop's Pond*

Age

Eyes too difficult to read have seen it all;
she stares from a knowing dark space

the folds of glow and shade settle in her lines
and she shines in his illumination.

She could be anybody's mother:
one who would scold at a misplaced collar,

at yellowed lace in need of a dash and splash
of lye, one who would tenderly admonish the dim,

spend her life with sheets on bleaching grounds,
whose heart would be spread with pride,

who would guide the brush she made
as it swelled with the trembling water of life

so hers would not diminish in a shrinking
multiverse, but would sparkle in furrowed light.

Sheila Aldous

Rembrandt van Rijn: *An old Woman called 'The Artist's Mother'*

An Enigma Resolved

If I stare at you hard enough,
perhaps I can time-travel
through a wormhole
back to a day in 1504
when sitting for your portrait
was no longer a novelty.

Your weekly visits
had continued for more than a year
and you'd grown to loathe the smell of turps.
You settled yourself in a wooden chair,
tucked a faded velvet cushion
behind the small of your back,

sighed and arranged your hands
the way he liked them,
right over left.
At first you tried making conversation
but he seemed more interested
in the skulls on his shelves.

So you emptied your mind,
sank into soporific silence,
waited for the hours to slide away.
The weight of centuries
pressed down on you,
squeezed the air from your lungs.

No sound but the clock
and Leonardo's slipper'd feet
shuffling back and forth.
Nothing of interest at all
until you saw, on the wall,
a fly struggling in a web

and almost smiled.

Kelly Davis

Leonardo da Vinci: *Mona Lisa*

Blonde

What you don't remember is the way
she fades to smudge, to mono-
chrome, to feint, to whiteout.

You don't forget the yellow hair,
the slash of a carmine mouth,
that charcoal edge, the turquoise

lids that match the wings
of a stand-up collar; or the clash
of tangerine behind the linctus

pink of skin. There she is,
twice five times five, all half-
closed eyes and kiss-me pout,

a set of flick-book movie stills,
again, again and over, nothing
changing but the colours.

What shocks you now is not
acrylic zing or canvas weave,
the irony of mock-naive repeat,

it's what you see you had
forgotten: all that shadow,
its hide and seek, its chill.

Susan Utting

Andy Warhol: *Marilyn Diptych*

Urchins

Boss-eyed, snaggle-toothed bedheads,
unwashed Raggedy Anns, you can
almost smell them, hear their Glesca patter.
The life jumps out of the canvas,
you see them, no longer part of the graffiti,
captured in a still life, but running
down the street, pushing the weans
in the bedraggled old pram, shouting insults
at each other, fidgeting in front of the lady,
waiting for the sketching to be over,
the pennies in their hands.
Van Gogh's black and white
village girl hasn't their street smarts,
you can't see her screeching from a
close mouth*, she is a different kind
of shy, a different kind of beautiful.
Joan's urchins think the lady's
crazy, but know a good thing when
they see it, and pennies means
fewer slaps from Maw, maybe
a fish supper for tea, a peaceful
few hours, before Paw brings
mayhem home from the pub.

Rosemary McLeish

*Close mouth – entrance to a tenement

Joan Eardley: *Children and Chalked Wall*

Night Music

You can lock the doors, even
bolt the air, but there's no way
of keeping your daughters in at night.
It doesn't matter how old they are –
three or four, six or seven –
a tornado throws them down the path
and ravishes them.
Stars glint like metal in their hair.
The darkness, fine as artists' ink,
seeps into their night clothes.
If you follow them down the path –
you turn to stone.

Then long after the midnight hour
the wind flings them back into the hallway
and up onto the landing
with its cracked green paint.
Their blouses open up like curtains
on their narrow, childish chests.

Your daughters grow giant sunflowers
in the gloom.
Their hair streams upwards
thick as cypress trees.

Moniza Alvi

Dorothea Tanning: *Eine Kleine Nachtmusik*

Through Her Eyes

Yellow shine of a low sun or of electric light
perhaps, rich colours of the rug, the book's
vividly patterned page-ends. Normally so pale
even his long nose and cheeks and intricate ear
are warmly tinted. She first tried to kill
herself before he died, because a world without
him was not liveable. She loved to look
at him, drew and painted him over and over
always like this, reading and reclined.

But it was his mind or soul, what made him
him, that she loved most and needed like an element,
the quickness in the eyes, the quirk of lips,
the expressiveness of his spider limbs.
Even in dreams, if she came upon a sudden wonder
she turned in her head at once to him.
It was his watchfulness that intrigued
her, and what he saw through his particular
looking: the play of his mind on it like light on water.

The book he holds in his golden fingers is shut
but his thoughts are inside it. This is a picture
of contemplation: his and the artist's
whose eyes followed him always. He is intent behind
the mask of lenses, the patriarchal
stern-seeming beard that was as soft as moss.
She has caught the glory of his hand. You understand
that she wanted to die first because she could not bear
to see it still, cold, changed into marble.

Chris Considine

Dora Carrington: *Portrait of Lytton Strachey*

Homecoming

And suddenly they are streaming back from the dead,
unburying themselves,
their tombstones mere props for gossip
now the final day has come.

Only this is not the last day,
but the first of an eternal summer
where loss turns back into desire,
for what can match the pleasure of a kiss
on the tongue of those grown accustomed to tasting nothing?

Nothing more glorious for those whose senses were lost
than these arms around the loved one's shoulder,
the conjugal embrace, the breasts
that never bruise with too much touching,
the heavy angels spilling out of windows and doors
to welcome them home.

This is what they dreamt of ascending to –
gardens, allotments, lamps pooling light over dinner.
This what they longed to recapture –
reaching round a chest that rises and falls,
the rapture of breath that doesn't stop.

Flesh ripe with joy now they are touching again –
lovers, mothers, children, fathers, plumped-up wives –
in this light that is never switched off,
these bodies that cannot have enough of each other,
this love that is always being made.

Rosie Jackson

Stanley Spencer: *The Resurrection: Reunion*

33

At the Window, Waiting

She stands
owned by a locked landscape
snow trees mist

The stillness of eternity

She dreams
a green frock an open window
a crowding of ship's masts

The expectation of love

Joy Howard

Vilhelm Hammershøi: *Interior, Woman at the Window*
Carl David Friedrich: *Woman at a Window*

Blue Profiles

My dream mate, we are twin souls;
we tangoed in harmony.
But salad days are fleeting,
green now shifts to memory.

As life curls at the edges,
we turn to face each other;
you mirror every blue move.
Love, let us age together.

Debjani Chatterjee

Anujan Ezhikode: *Leaf Series #2*

Contradiction

I am the two-faced bride
rose-smiling under my veil
demure, eyes half-shut.
Uncovered, in another place
I expose my breast, swear
and fight, sing from deep
inside, fish the night,
search bars for a man
tattooed with flames,
savour wormwood.
I can be all loneliness
and fall in darkness.
Open-eyed I follow
any saxophone and drum
to broken and crimson light.
With the sun I'm again
a virgin, the moon becomes
just a rolling marble.
With day I rise to float
through my cobalt world.
A child, I clutch carnations,
whisper small words, feel
my ribbons tight, too tight
for this sort of restlessness.

Jenny Morris

Marc Chagall: *La Mariée à Double Face*

Lot's Daughters

When was it the scarlet folds of our dresses
became flames, igniting our hearts?
We remember the night angels came to our house
(those dark eyes, those beautiful hands),
how men clamoured at the door to sleep with them
and our father offered our bodies instead.

We remember the silence:
one moment our mother weeping,
fretting for all we'd left behind:
her jars of scented oils, the little grey cat.
Then she was gone, emptiness,
no sound of her, and our father
shouting we mustn't look back.
Salt tears, sulphur from the burning city
rasped our tongues. A column
of absence shivered between us.

Resting on the green hillside,
one of us pours wine into a cup,
the other strokes our father's head –
the only man left for us.
Somehow we must be mothers.

Now we understand why our mother
turned her face away.

Penny Ayers

Lucas Cranach the Elder: *Lot and his Daughters*

In Sansepolcro

Surely your donors weren't expecting you –
archaic, majestic, challenging every notion
of a patriarchal god.

Not Mary, submissive to divine commands
but Artemis, protector of women and the young
your demeanour shows you've seen all this before.

Supplicants huddle under your cloak
begging protection from the plague
there's something touching in their trust.

Fear ripples across upturned faces
at the black-robed presence
they pretend they cannot see
refusing to believe there's nowhere to hide.

Verity Schanche

Piero della Francesco: *The Madonna of Mercy*

silent shapes

Aldeburgh Beach

Sky falls through carved spaces to form the words
I hear those voices that will not be drowned
edging the loneliest scallop shell in England.
Fishing boats and buoys flicker on the nearby
deep; my feet kick empty cans which jar
against the rumble of shifting pebbles.

I trace my way across this crinkled steel,
its fanlike folds cold beneath my hands,
and find myself in the hinge of the clam
anchored in the midst of shingle,
where yellow-horned poppies grow sturdy
and ragwort, thistle and sea-kale thrive.

Eleanor J Vale

Maggi Hambling: *The Scallop*

Set in Stone

See where marble fell away,
revealing at its heart
the world's core: for here
this body broken for us all
is muscled in stone, veined
where rock itself pulses, wrapped
in petrified folds.

Look further: see beyond pale flesh
and focus where a mother's downcast gaze
pierces the soul's centre. Let her grief
start tears behind your eyes
as if your son – scourged, tortured, crucified –
freezes in your arms.

This moment encapsulates eternity,
fixes the cost of reconciliation;

and it is here, where sightless eyes angle
through neverending pain, you learn
the strength of woman.

Her hands that fed and dressed the child
support his wounded side, gesture
a need to understand. Her lap,
where an infant smiled, cradled safe,
holds his dead weight. Her lips
that kissed away his tears are set,
closed firm against a hint
of pity or complaint.

She is unyielding; her power is absolute
and incorruptible. Look again
where woman's essence stirs the very air,
to see where marble weeps and bleeds.

Alison Chisholm

Michelangelo: *Pietà*

Muses

I am drawn to sculptures
in large white spaces,
small faces mostly

and not of Greek gods,
but silent shapes that
draw you in: marble

or bronze – Brancusi –
those creatures with curves,
slopes, possibly mouths,

it was hard to tell,
walking around them
watching them sleep –

like my daughters, newborn,
in their clean plastic cots
at the hospital

absolutely themselves
and worthy of entire
fascination.

Susanna Harding

Constantin Brâncuşi: *Heads*

43

Awakening

You made her of acacia,
a wooden woman
slender as a tree,
the grain describing
belly, breast and hips,
a navel where the knotting
used to be.

Silent she stands alone
abandoned here,
a forlorn, lifeless figure
on the floor,
exposed to the relentless
searching eyes,
stripping her bare,
revealing node and flaw.

What if her hibernating
dryad heart
should wake at a sudden sound,
begin to beat
and buds begin to form
upon her hands
while tangled roots
extend her twitching feet.

What if she split
her shiny outer case
and from her navel
grew a branching tree
and leaves unfurled
along her aching spine
and ivy twisted up
her creaking knee.

Then she would stretch
her branching arms and dance
and weave a pattern
in the forest air,

a maze of steps
as ancient as the woods,
a storm of blossom
bursting in her hair.

Jenny Pritchard

Ossip Zadkine: *Vénus*

Under a Beech at Brantwood

In a clearing stands a wooden sculpture,
its slender arm and open hand, offering.

Birds perch to drink from its palm,
peck insects from its crevices.

If I were to sit as quiet and still as this tree,
believe myself to be part of everything,

would birds eat from my hand too,
sit and sing at my fingertips?

Barbara Hickson

John Ruskin's house, Coniston Water

Interlocked

From cold stone feel the heat of lovers' fire,
where, in a sinuous trance, two bodies curl.
He holds her close, one hand under her hair,
one on her thigh. Arced back, their forms dovetail;
her arm is raised, one breast in his arm's crook
and both have closed their eyes, as scent and touch
drown out all else. They have no need to look,
abandoned as they are to passion's clutch.

Outside the window a fine net is spread
over a quadrangle. Two birds lie there,
so ragged, hunched and still they're clearly dead,
so close they might have been a mating pair.
Impossible to say if these two doves
became entangled in the coils of love.

Jean Watkins

Robert Gibbings: *The Embrace*

The Ain Sakhri Lovers

Little bean, twin cotyledon, lips ajar –
He is embracing her, or she him.
Their faces are hidden from us. His knees,
Arched under hers, open her, a flower.

How beautiful they are, flawless, nameless,
Older than writing, than building, and tender
And delicate; for he has taken root
In her, or she in him, and they are gone

Into the greater, all-embracing stillness.
Born out of the one grain, they are a secret
Known only to each other, almost worn
Back to the pebble, polished, smoothed in water,

Or deep in the furrow, or on the plain's tongue –
And plucked, for this moment, out of the long river.

Katrina Porteous

11,000 year old sculpture from the Ain Sakhri caves near Bethlehem

Dancer

Was it too much
to ask a dancer to stop
long enough to capture her
in cold, hard bronze?
Here she is, foot poised
longing to step
down from the plinth,
to float her long arms
wafting air towards us
to kick and stretch legs
into gracious lengths.
With a tiny twist at the waist
she turns to us, uncovered,
saying I too know how it is
to be caught, curtailed.

Anne Eccleshall

Henri Gaudier-Brzeska: *Dancer*

The Artist's Model Daydreams

My head is a spoon that dips and scoops
fine sugar from a china bowl, remembers
sherbet ochre tongues and the stain on the
tip of a finger shrivelled with sucking.

My face is a flower that turns with the sun
sneaks a look from the edge of a tarmac square,
remembers the scrape and bounce of fivestone chalks
worn smooth and round with playing.

My back is an S that aches on a stool, remembers
the scale of ascending C where thumbs go under,
the broken key and the ring of a fender, bruised
in simple time, by a poker's four-four beating.

My legs are a longcase clock, a pendulum pair
that swings and remembers great aunt afternoons
the rub of a cut-moquette settee, a glimpse
of a beaded muslined jug, and ticking.

Susan Utting

Alberto Giacometti: *Girl Dreaming*

Her Name

She is called
   after a bird
      of the night
         but she is an otter
            dressed in summer blue
               dressed in riverbank
            dressed in leafblade
         sedge and dragonfly.
      She stands on a black plinth
      her forepaws on her belly
like hands. Her tail is protective.
Golden eyelids cover
shuttered eyes as she
dreams of owls. Her
   golden nose is raised
   points towards yews
      and cypresses
         reaching for the scent
            of owls. She has come
               a long way from the river
                  but she carries it with her
                     along with its memory
               of the ruby call
                        of owls

Jennie Osborne.

Claire Scully: *Bejewelled Owl*

50

Body of Work

This lyre of yourself

this stringed bronze
plucked to your tune
thought transformed
transforming
harmony created
from movement.

Beneath its patina
the carved lines hold
a cradling of light

This inward eye

searches us.
This looking
looking again
　　　　becomes our looking
space revealed, concealed
an inner landscape.

This touchstone

of revelations
form, colour, markings
that give life
　　　　embrace living
and human spirit.

This celebration

that speaks
from earth
of sea, of land
of sky-wide light.

Josie Walsh

Barbara Hepworth: *Sculpture with Colour and Strings*

51

Rubble-woman

Your neck is a segment of column,
your headscarf, a terracotta helmet.
The basalt apron is your armour.

You were once a shop,
a hospital, a chapel.
You were lintel and hearth.

Your gloveless hands are bloodied
from pick-and-hammer labour,
scraping and hacking at bricks.
Watches have been stolen – hours,
years are tapped, stack by stack.

Brokenness. Intolerable
smoking beauty of ruins
against cold blue sky.

If I were to stroke your cheek,
and a fragment chipped off,
I doubt you could weep.
If another fire poured down,
would dust-words
spurt from your lips?

Bombs lie low.
The dead are old.
Lilac blossoms
in a courtyard.

Cellared after dusk.
Your forever work –
you mosaic your son
together – the lapis
tesserae of his eyes.

Anne Ryland

Max Lachnit: *Trümmerfrau* (Mosaic bust pieced together from the rubble of Dresden
after the firestorm).

Reconfiguration

After Gallipoli
the Somme

the sculptor
      attacked
            his paean
                  to progress
                        industry
                              virility

      tore apart limbs
            formed art's amputee –
speaking
            to men broken by war
      creative flesh
                  mangled by machinery.

Liz Parkes

Jacob Epstein: *Torso in Metal from the Rock Drill*

53

It's Never Too Late

One night when the tide is full and the moon
is neon bright, I'll go to Crosby Beach, shed
anxieties and clothes, wade until my toes
can't feel the sand. I'll throw myself onto the waves
and plough a liquid furrow to the furthest rusty shape.
He'll blink surprise and with a mighty breath, crack
the barnacles from his chest. Creaking, he'll flex
his right arm then his left, both knees. Encrustations
will shower off to dint the surface of the sea.
He'll look at me and smile. In synchrony
we'll turn, begin to power arms and scissor legs.
We'll leave behind the orange glows of Bootle,
Birkenhead, freestyle our way past Ynys Môn
into the starry darkness of the Irish Sea.

Gill Learner

Anthony Gormley: *Another Place*

Recovery Stroke

How heavy it seems, this duck in flight,
wing down and flattened, not knowing

if it will have the strength to pull up again,
waiting for the next push forwards,

a divine acrobat – comical at times
stuck on the wall in threes

as if there is something quite absurd,
ridiculous, about a duck in flight,

but look at its beauty:
every feather and tendon

used to the maximum in its rotation
of back and forth, up and down,

knowing without being told
that moving forward

requires a moving back,
that no stroke is wasted –

that the greatest beauty sometimes
happens at the weakest point.

Rosie Jackson

Grainger McKoy: *Recovery Wing*

About Time

Twenty-nine years I sprawled outside the gallery
after Moore chose me – me! – as his tour de force.

Neither naked nor draped in the stuff Leeds made
and sells, my Jane Austen eyes miss nothing.

I watched a generation sidle, cycle, wait
for the 81, prod sandwiches, play phone games, flirt.

I watched the clouds, the fog, the Town Hall clock
tick round. I watched the night-shift cleaners come

and go. Whatever the old man meant, I know
I sit for the rest they earned, their elbow grease,

the hurriers' and housemaids' knees, the centuries
of broken backs that made Leeds great.

A crane came once: six hard-hats swung me up
over The Headrow to Amsterdam for a stint

on the Rijksmuseum lawn, where I reclined
with the best. Gleaming, graffitied, blown on,

snowed on, shat on, spat on. See sex in me
if you want, young man, but don't underestimate

these wall-high hips, these pit-prop biceps.
Stick your head here, sunshine, at your own risk.

This long-fingered hand can weave, can write,
can strum, can calibrate – and this left fist can fight.

Spreading my bulk as if Leeds were an Eden,
I claim my place in the city's pantheon.

Julia Deakin

Henry Moore: *Reclining Woman*

the pulse of us

Ensemble

A clarinet's clear voice weaves
           among violins, cello and viola
silver keys shining on black wood,

threads its sound to lead
           follow and encircle
warp and weft of strings,

rises above and dips below
           traces patterned intricacies
while four bows flow and flicker.

The reed's high notes expand
           and soften, touch
a melody and mood in me.

Jane Monach

W A Mozart: *Clarinet Quintet*

Epiphany

The needle clicks, the speaker splutters, and chords
burst out of the radiogram, splashing on to the carpet,
the ashtray of Woodbine butts, the television jaunty
on splayed legs, my green school skirt and falling down socks.
I let myself be swept on to the sofa, rinsed by the music
of the composer who strode round Vienna half-pissed,
scratching at the lice under his wig, dashing to the privy
in between scratching storm clouds and joy on to paper.
With a groan I let my head fall back and float, my hair
a diadem streaming around my head, until I am washed up
on the red cushions when the adagio empties the ocean of
all but crystalline drops, each one tender as the kitten face
of a viola. The cat yawns, offering her dusty belly to the sun.

Caroline Gilfillan

Ludwig van Beethoven: *Piano Concerto No 5 'The Emperor'*

Merry-go-round

Round goes a melody, merry as hens pecking,
strings swing like girls holding hands,
until the weave begins, and cloth unrolls,
and there in front of you is a bolt of continuous silk
which has become a Truth.
The music
(no sooner come than gone)
cannot be questioned,
because it is defined by its going;
the sounds are beautiful
not because they start,
nor even while they hang in air:
the beauty is in the not-ness,
of each note and chord having gone for ever.

Each swell, each scale, legato change, and dance and swing from
note to note,
from chord to chord,
says, 'Here I am – I was' – and in the space
between 'I am not yet'
and 'Though I was, I am no more'
is a shape, solid and confident:

the world is everything that was the case.

Hermione Sandall

Alexander Zemlinsky: *Lyric Symphony*

63

Painting the Harmonies

When you say this chord, or that, is brilliant,
do you mean that it excites, being
made up of moving sounds
– pitches, timbres –
that tintinnabulate upon the ear,
fleetingly shifting, cascading, glittering
time-lapsed ice crystals
bejewelling a leaf?

Or do you mean that chords are
topaz with chrysoprase with scarlet,
or jasper, sapphire, chalcedony, colours of the walls
of the New Jerusalem, or the marvellous flash
of green between red and red?

Or do we speak of the same things?

Mandy Macdonald

Olivier Messiaen: *Couleurs de la Cité Céleste*

Ambush

It has to be November
and I'm ambushed
by Mendelssohn
the violin concerto
old favourite
I skip over these days.

I'm clutching the pine table
find myself staring
at rain pouring from a choked gutter
an old cloth
abandoned in the yard
grey as the day.

I want to rescue it
wring out dirty water
wring out Mendelssohn's notes
and pain in some deep part I can't name

change the music to Pachelbel or Bach
something that believes
in a pattern,
get back to clean and white again.

Jennie Osborne

Felix Mendelssohn: *Violin Concerto*

Fair Isle Fugue

'It's knitting music' says Jack, stumbling, age seven,
into the world of baroque, and workmanlike
he grins, the unknown rendered once more known.
Not for him white-water rafting screaming towards
stillness, mathematical ecstasies skidding to solutions.

Rather a perfect eighty crotchets to the inch;
the marshalled ribbing of development,
then sailing free into plain and purl, new
patterns ushered in, and then receding.

He hears the long wool twisting melody;
knows it sturdy, useful as his new jumper;
perfect for purpose, holding together, each note
linked above, below, in space, in time.

Then all cast-off, the last stitch neatly looped.

Pat Simmons

J S Bach: *The Art of the Fugue*

Tonus Peregrinus in Notre Dame

Perhaps it's Latin
for the way a thrush mixes tones
as she flits to the tree, perfecting
the scent of uncertain fruits,
lifting opals from water-palaces,
spooling *differencias*,
filling the beat with honey drops.

Or the way the girl dodges quick
from bar to bus station
swinging long hair, wearing new prints
of tiny flowers, patchouli in the air,
glances over at the local boy.

But now it's doubled, *organum*, straight lined,
a hand in the dark tugging its ghost along.
There's a kite on a string,
a belly chime gathers and swings
and the voice bells vibrate and wandering
goes dominus dominus dom dom om

enormous body of symphony combines
and seals play, whales play
in unmeasured cumulative memory

where time slows in the clerestory
and sight comes sharp and clear
like a small bird caught in the throat
circling close and closer to the O.

Pamela Coren

Léonin: *Viderunt Omnes, Magnus Liber Organi*

Rose

From this white light
silver-blue voices flow,
it deflects its tiered colours,
the music of the spheres.

Silky to the touch, it forms a shape,
a circle, a silver rose,
a perfect flower, multifoliate,
the song petalled, azure tipped.

It lulls towards death:
yet the dead are loud,
they walk my mind at night,
their words, steps, slaps are lively.

Thelma Laycock

Arvo Pärt: *Lamentate – Da Pacem Domine*

Soundings

a quick mouse path of music
running through the tall stems
of violins

                    clouds gather
in the bellies of cellos
rain spatters
black and white washed
                    pebbles

bees flood
from the hill of the hive
lift the kilt
of a song

breath
fingers
ink
and all our ears
          opening like oysters
in a stream of sound

                    how
we are all strings
strung in one gut
and at the last
                    one heart.

Kate Foley

Sally Beamish: *Piano Concerto No 1 'Hill Stanzas'*

Song Without Words

'White birds flying against a terrible black sky': Anna Akhmatova

So runs the song

Skeins of geese headed
home   singing into
the wind
        a wind set to
hurl off course
pluck out feathers   scour
to dust

so it goes

An armful of doves   flung
by an old air   high
above town
        the town that is
reaching for guns
to scatter in smithereens   sling
on dunghills

so it goes

Skimming swans hymn
a misty chorale
        but frost   hard frost comes
to petrify wingsails
nail down webbed feet   deal death
at dawn

So runs the song
so it goes   *so*

Joy Howard

Dmitri Shostakotich: *Symphony No 11 'The Year 1905'*

70

Winter

A dove flies through

swallowed by stars
    palls of wood-smoke   remains
       of an evening

that entered a young girl's dreams
    with love
       and flakes of snow stealing

         red and green from hillsides

Above   air barely breathes
    between pines gloved
       in wintersong

Below the surface   smooth as promises
    bones hide   aching
       in the darkest truth   tolling
          old age   sliding

around beds of moss
    stones   lodged   slow   deep
       as December blood in sleeping fish

The surface holds   gleams
    strings of tinsel   keeping
       then   and   now   apart

Too late to skate on   I watch it melt
    like a broken heart   finding its way
       through the years

         traces in ice
            drifting   free

Kerry Darbishire

Joni Mitchell: *River*

At Dawn

The lake makes a disc of itself.
Then mist rises in spirals
close to the water.

> A breeze makes a wave and a wave and a wave.
> No doubt the water is cold. The air too.
> This is a small hours' lake.

And I remember Sinatra, a voice
like a reed, how it floated and lingered.
And I think of the time when

> sorting things, I discarded L.P.s.
> even the one, curved by strong sun
> when it lay for a day, on that table in Clapham.

That voice on the vinyl
that could take over-used words
restoring their shine

> in lyrics and strings, that mapped
> some in-between state, like mist
> or the earliest sun, on a lake.

Josie Walsh

Mann and Hilliard: *In the Wee Small Hours of the Morning*

72

Jazz Among the Scones

If pints were Pernods
and afternoon were night,
if this bright room were a cellar
and neat rows of chairs a shamble,
if iced fancies were amandes salées
and fresh air a fog of Gitanes,
we would be there, we would,
at the Hot Club de Paris
in berets and shades, but
snell winds whip the granite
so we keep on our coats
for the concert, too cold
to be cool.

Then they strike up and we
are aflame. Timeless jazz and memories
of the perfect pair, gypsy and fiddler.
Our Django is a lanky Scot,
Stéphane G sports a dainty dress.
They embrace us in thrumming chords
and joyous violin, in compelling beats
and dancing notes, the thrilling rhythms
and improvisations pure delight.
They swing, we swing and we are there,
really there, at the Hot Club. Cool.

Marka Rifat

At the Carmelite Hotel, Aberdeen

Finding My Way Home

Am I meant to hold my breath
as the violin strings pull taut?
It leaves me without
oxygen – a balloon deflated
as after a dance and no-one
asks to see me home.

It's my long suffering, worrying
father who met me from the last bus,
knowing I would want an arm
to lean on as I descended the hill,
heels too high, to our home.

Now I have nobody to inflate
my lungs except myself.
I hurry, cast my nets until
an arm, or cheek or eye meets
with approval, and this
isn't one CD too many, and to hear
that violin teetering on those
torturous notes, cannot cause a catastrophe,
and start the whole father longing
business up again.

Pauline Hawkesworth

Sibelius: *Violin Concerto No.1*

Listening On the Train

Starts quietly. How does silence
become sound? And then you see you're moving,
see before feeling. A beginning
looks to an end, the subject of this work.

But though the words speak of death, the music
sings of life – germinates, bursts out lush
and unstoppable as spring in a southern country.
Voices swoop and curl around each other.

All the sweetness of life: love, elation, heat,
the large and small enjoyments, beauty
of sky and land in fragments flashing across,
faster, more rhythmical as we pick up speed.

Beyond the glass the world outlasts our passing.
Like a musical note our noise is here – gone –
even the echo of us. Look now! On one side, light,
on the other, mounting darkness. Lux aeterna

luceat eis ne cadant in obscurum. Lux aeterna –
the horror of it. Imagine – like arctic midsummer
but much brighter – blazing all day, all night – snowblindness,
seablindness (skirting now the white flare of the ocean).

Yes, give me rest, eternal rest – a proper deep, deep
sleep at last, but in utter dark with no stray ray of streetlamp
or passing car. Not even the yellowish twilight
of this train as it approaches its final destination.

Chris Considine

Giuseppe Verdi: *Requiem*

75

Concerto

In the deeps a slow to and fro to and fro
rocks the long swells into watery hills

lumbering landward a rush onto beach
where frost catches spray on the wave-crest

and droplets of ice from the far north
rasp on pebbles like hail on glass.

Earth wakes cold lungs breathe out a long wind
white waves thrash at dark sky

and far below the continuo a slow
to and fro to and fro the pulse of us

the swell and the surge of the sea
in the blood of a born-and-bred inlander

Joy Howard

Igor Rachmaninov: *Piano Concerto No 2*

Bach at St Davids

In spring, fifteen centuries ago,
the age of saints, and stones, and holy wells,
a blackbird sang its oratorio
in the fan-vaulted canopy of the trees,
before Bach, before walls, before bells,
cantatas, choirs, cloisters, clerestories.

The audience holds its breath when the soprano,
like a bird in the forest long ago,
sings the great cathedral into being,
and apse to nave it calls back, echoing,
till orchestra and choir in harmony
break on the stones like the sea.

And listen! Out there, at the edge of spring,
among the trees, a blackbird answering.

Gillian Clarke

J S Bach: *Cantatas*

wearing an alternative skin

Makeshift

No still explosions here; no rocks
or concentric shocks, though the chance
that lichens may grow and spread
seems high in this moist green room
where ventilation is confined to shortness
of breath, and since the nurses can't attend,

it's down to us dear friend. You've been
considered and sometimes pragmatical;
though surprisingly amenable to the assaults
of time. Now close your eyes against
the sting of shooting stars or suds;
while I try to tame this shower snake.

Allow your tongue to search the parched
terrain of lips for dreamed-of mango juice
and rejoice in clean hair before we are
chastised for the puddled floor; you assaulted
with needles and polythene; I sent away,
sorry and battered as that famous tin basin.

Wendy Klein

Elizabeth Bishop: *The Shampoo*

Overnight in a Hotel

The stone building in the old part of town
survived two wars. The cobbled street
may be named *Boulanger* or *Petite Bourrée*.
The windows give views of the river,
yellow streetlamps, a thin layer of snow.

You wait in that room for a phone to ring.

Your thoughts will be laid to rest
in wingback chairs with subtle checks.
A row of robust coat-hangers catches
sadness, guilt and shame: pearly buttons,
plain trousers, creased linen jacket.

Each dream includes that small compass.
Its trembling red needle showing you
there will always be a way home.

Fokkina McDonnell

Thomas Tranströmer: *Homewards*

Head Full of Birds

He would have humming-birds,
I would have sparrows,
knitting my hair
into Gordian knots.

He would have green doves,
I would have collared,
too-tooing 'I-love-you'
loud in my ear.

Let them fly in my head,
let them perch on my brow,
nestle like warmth
in the cups of my ears –

the chaffinch, the robin,
the dunnock, the thrush –

a tangle of feathers
and claws in my hair,
a fury of wings
disturbing the air.

Gill McEvoy

Pablo Neruda: *Cabeza a Pájaros*

The Yearly Trick

I walk the graveyard in deep snow,
listening to muffled echoes – the slow
drip drop of water from overhanging
branches, the distant hoot and rattle
of trains, the cawing of a crow
in flight, rasping its leitmotif
across the valley. Though winter bites
the earth and seeks to tighten its hold,
though March is cold and sunlight brief,
the trees are coming into leaf.

The sky, an unrelenting grey,
shrouds what still remains of day
in an impenetrable gloom.
And yet, beneath my feet, something
is shifting, stretching, stirring the clay.
Like Lazarus rising from the dead,
the earth discards its cerements.
New twigs are springing into life,
their green tips arching overhead
like something almost being said.

Beyond the cemetery gate
where rows of ancient oaks await
the end of winter, I climb the stile
that leads me back to childhood woods.
I walk its paths, investigate
a snowdrop thrusting its pallid head
through frozen earth, piercing the shroud
of white. Camellias, too, are striving,
beginning to show faint hints of red.
The recent buds relax and spread.

A wind from the antipodes
breathes life into the forest. The trees
are quivering with an age-old song
that speaks of hope and of despair,
of summer's warmth and winter's freeze.

Nothing can shake their firm belief
that all rebirth requires a death.
Deep down they know the bitter truth –
their finery is all too brief,
their greenness is a kind of grief.

Doreen Hinchliffe

Philip Larkin: *The Trees*

Another Web

It only takes a day to
build another web in
undisturbed corners
where the orb-weaver
waits, promising to
love you like a spider
loves a fly.

Silk-wrapped child
the wind cries, leave
though spider silk is
strong you're light
enough to fall.
Small wings are all
you need.

Ness Owen

Walt Whitman: *A Noiseless Patient Spider*

Winchester

This soft September day
in clean, sharp air
I followed his footsteps

past the Cathedral, the college,
the city gates, to that ancient place
they call Saint Cross.

I walked by the meadows
by the clear river
where cornfields winnowed

like a woman's hair.
Autumn has always been
a woman for me too:

The loaded bough,
drowsy bees, falling leaves,
the show of poppies.

I say, forget 'spoilt spring'
the shrill music of mating;
perpetual love calls,

give me a choir of swallows,
mournful cries of grown lambs;
the song of the robin.

Denise Bennett

John Keats: *Ode to Autumn*

Another World to Walk In

I'm on a journey to a night class
in my hand a hold-all full of poetry,
my legs carry me down the hill to a bus,
I feel tired, vulnerable, concerned
by the demolition of a nearby house,

then, travelling on the underground,
I see, above the window in the train,
blazing out on white, black is printed:
  I stepped from plank to plank
  A slow and cautious way...
I marvel at it, write it down, I learn it,

so, when I miss the bus that drives
through woodland trees, up a winding lane,
I hold the poem I've copied open,
begin to say the words:
  The stars about my head I felt
  About my feet the sea...

After the class, and waiting now, alone,
the haunting iambs, like a beating heart,
lead me to remember words half-learned,
buried underneath the evening, and

when outside the station, in the July dark, I wait
tired, anxious for the bus home:
  I know not but the next
  Could be my final inch:
following the metre like a thread,
these last lines come:
  This gave me that precarious gait
  Some call Experience.

Sara Boyes

Emily Dickinson: *I Stepped from Plank to Plank*

Reflection

What is she really? An old woman
– or terrible fish? I am a lake,
unmisted by love or dislike.
No preconceptions, not cruel,
I swallow immediately. Each day
she bends over me, searching
my reaches with tears, an agitation of hands.
Most of the time I meditate. The moon,
darkness, separate us, over and over.

Has she drowned a young woman?
Cruel! Whatever. It is the face
of the young woman that replaces
the moon's silver each pink morning.
I have looked at it so long, I think
it is part of my heart. Day
after day the old woman comes,
searches my flickers with the eye
of a little god – or terrible fish.

Rosemary Doman

Sylvia Plath: *Mirror*

Old Crow

Or maybe this was
the way of it

maybe she saw
the rainbow radiance
sheening the wings

or lusted
for a sword-sharp bill
an anthracite eye

maybe she longed
for a high-branched haven
the clasp of a horned claw

or – as a woman will
under whatever moon –

she glimpsed you
lit and shining
and took you for hers

Joy Howard

R S Thomas: *The Way of It*

89

Sad Litany

Assorted characters of death and blight
surround me now, I count them off, sad
litany of loss, like the ingredients of a mad
witches' broth. Fill a glass, hold it to the light
watch a snowdrop spider and a moth fight
it out, as you and I do, now what we had
has gone. How did it happen, my golden lad?
We were so ready to begin the morning right.

What but design of darkness to appall?
Yet white dominates, moths struggle in the night
song birds fall silent as harsh corncrakes call
I count dead flowers from an albino heal-all.

Can design govern random things so small?

Angela Kirby

Robert Frost: *Design*

A Sevenling

I loved three things about him
his shoulders, his laugh
and his long kisses

I hated his wild rages and his lies
the way he criticised my driving
that he always had to win

Now he sleeps beneath the snow

Angela Kirby

Anna Akhmatova: *He Loved Three Things*

Dusk

1

What is it about these blue abrasions
of light falling as dusk across the page,

are they shared now with other poets
in other rooms? You will have us reach

for light, lean over your shoulder
to touch dusk in another place

as if it were sand wearing an alternative
skin. Reaching for language abrades

the fingertips lightly like braille.
You could run your fingers

over the page and find that ache
of things ending

2

There is grace in November's passing;
the hill I can see from my window

re-bones itself, its arc backlit.
Racks and scuds of cloud follow rain

and dusk comes early.
Somewhere you are writing and have

marked the unbearable permanence
of stone how its curve catches

the breath its folds darken and
include you. Outside leaves

are falling, the beech is
unadorned and plain.

Janet Sutherland

Eavan Boland: *The Rooms of Other Women Poets*

Snow

I hate all films that start with snow,
Christmas schmaltz the lot of them:
Bambi, Love Story, Frozen.

The cynical director, his assistant
with the snow machine
blowing fluffy cotton-wool flakes

to muffle the cries of motherless fawn,
orphaned little girls in castles,
a young wife breathing her last.

I've nothing against a good cry
and I'll make an exception
for Doctor Zhivago and the ice palace

where Yuri will make a fresh start
despite the wolves, will write poems
in fingerless gloves, ice on his moustache,

even though I know it won't end well,
that she'll step into the fur-lined sleigh,
that he'll breathe a hole in the ice for one last look.

Carole Bromley

Don Paterson: *Rain*

Appearances

From an upstairs room it looks as though
a snowdome's been upturned before my eyes.
Beyond a field of yellowing winter grass,
behind a scrawled hedge and three leafless trees
inked on the brown and distant wooded hill
my gaze is caught and held. I'm mesmerised.
Everything is changing all the time
as I watch the hundreds of white shapes
fall and rise the far side of the trees.

Sun strikes white, a flashing blizzard swirls,
then as they flicker down and disappear
I know that they are gulls; my view alters.
Nothing stays. The trees lose all their starkness.
There's more than trees between snowbirds and me.

Jo Peters

Louis McNeice: *Snow*

93

Exhibition

A young woman looks in her hand mirror
and in the mirror there's always a secret

She sees the warrior-archer Minamoto staring back.
He's so strong – even twenty of us cannot draw back his bow string

People are admiring the sacred pine tree
travellers from the city are asking local children for directions

Mount Fuji is everywhere
and over the mountain dawn is always breaking

Kites are flying in the dawn sky
Red Fuji Pink Fuji

Now there are eight different waterfalls
a frog hidden in a lily

the most beautiful ducks in the world,
small flowers, big flowers.

Various people are climbing the mountain.
A lion is a swirling mass of fur.

The lion dancer follows in his wake shaking his mane
for old man Hokusai and his daughter.

Joy Howard

Penelope Shuttle: *Hokusai*. A 'found'poem. All words and phrases are taken from the
original.

Making Our Own Garden

If this place here, without plant or flower, is a
garden, or we choose to call it so, then Nothing,
neither light nor rain can change it, and we
will remain exactly as we are, even if we were
growing only the idea of roses, what roses are,
preparing our bed, not for summer but for now,
without a trowel we could tend our minds and
flesh, harvesting pleasure from what won't ever
die or go to seed. A leafless arboretum shall
be our shade and shelter, and could also be
our greenhouse too, words sweetly blooming
from our lips, curling like vines, becoming the
hedge whip that will become the border. Nothing –
not next door's bindweed, not the leylandii or the
virulent bamboo will find its way inside where no
thing outside our own allotment grows. When one's
garden is one's own, there are no thorns upon the Rose.

Cheryl Moskowitz

Paul Celan: *Psalm*. A 'golden shovel' poem, where the last words of each line are
taken in order from the original.

Clydeside

where the Clyde broadens into lowtide mudflats –
as if Mungo himself had warned the waters
to shrink from dalliance with earthly things –
and wooden ribs fracture around the empty
hearts of sunken boats three times the size
of his skin-and-wicker coracle;

where the redcoat fortress topping Dumbarton Rock
peers over tidal flux, with the bored eyes
of retirement, at Greenock's white boxes
stacked tier on tier up the hill, at the docks
where cranes twiddle their thumbs;

where even pleasure boats have dwindled
to an endangered species, and the only ships –
war-grey frigates, rich men's megayachts,
floating holidays tall as hotels –
stop short miles from the centre, the *dear green place*
sold into the slavery of wealth,
Mungo's bones down in the vault fretful;

where the orange drum shouts in the streets down which
his clergy carried the Corpus Christi host;
where below tarmac old fields nurse their seeds
for good or ill, biding their time.

A C Clarke

Lavinia Greenlaw: *Blackwater*

Progression

We can start anywhere. We progress,
grow in years, and doing so, we find that the world
becomes stranger, the pattern more complicated
of dead and living.

There is a time for sunlit days, for the heat
that brightens our faces, for the singing and laughter
of love. Will the ashes be deciphered?
Love is most nearly itself when here and now
cease to matter;

difficult to imagine in the days of rushing lives,
difficult to imagine, impossible to put into words,
because one has only learnt to get the better of words.
Here or there does not matter, but perhaps
neither gain nor loss.

For us there is only the trying,
and the progression becomes harder. Old men
ought to be explorers, ought to feel the wonder,
feel the brightness of each new day,
the dawning, the progressing.
A lifetime burning in every moment.

Doris Corti

T S Eliot: *East Coker*

caught in that glance

Camera Obscura

When blinds are lowered in the chamber
    at the top of the medieval tower,
silence is drawn too, a breath-holding
    hush-in-the-dark expectation like a theatre,
or the eerie quieting of birds
    at the sprinting twilight of an eclipse –
their song unnoticed before, now unearthly
    in its absence – and then, as fast as the moon
passes over the face of the sun, the lens
    flings-wide on the camera, and the smoothwhite
viewing bowl floods with light-and-colour,
    so the people, ranged around it as if for a séance
or to hear the oracle, gasp-with-O-mouths
    at the everydaywonder of light, at the normal
cars on the street below, passing close-enough
    to touch, at the secret swimming-pools on roofs,
a woman hanging out washing,
    the world we walk through halfasleep;
like sometimes catching sight of yourself
    in a shopwindow and hardly recognizing her;
or glimpsing a tilt-of-a-head which reminds you
    how much you love someone; or swimming-out
and looking back at the curve-of-the-bay
    from the-prospect-of-the-sea, where
behindyou becomes beforeyou, the familiar houses
    and bars backtofront like looking-glass-land,
concave as the world in the bowl of a spoon.

Maggie Butt

Torre de los Perdigones, Seville

Parallax

alone in a darkened room
I am the camera
that is the eye
of the turning tower
Fernsehturm 2001

the restaurant revolves
unreeling the earth's curvature
diners drift into place
like astronauts
light pools in their raised glasses
voices fold over and over

outside
the high white dome of the rotunda
is awash with the deep breathing of the sea

sky streams across the screen
between two pillars
people arrive and leave
everything is composed
frame by frame

I have new eyes
each thing they light on
gathers urgency
undergoes transformation
I am the camera,
the rest is artwork
installation

I fling elation like a grappling hook
but no one pays attention
it does not take hold

no eye it seems can ever pierce
the absolute otherness
of the other

Elisabeth Rowe

Tacita Dean: *Berlin Works* at Tate St Ives 2005

Again

At first it is a single glowing cell
then two that meet and part; then three
red flames, budding and rippling up
through black. A lilting halo

mambos to music in a green star of shoots
then tilts to a sharpened wedge of pink
and marries it like a finger. A wisp of smoke
unlooses, swaying blue and luminous

as a bemused snake – then crankhandles out,
replaced by a pair of threads,
magenta turquoise flesh that interlocks
and swells and gives – withdraws

through swollen lips. A gold fruit rocks
in the wet crescent of the moon's mouth
and the snake uncoils, the glossy pulsing heart
has reproduced itself, the screen dividing

and dividing, each new-born square alive
to pump and dance and jiggle up down up
to split again, baroque
as a jumping quilt – and fades

to a pair of chalky smears first blue
then red-green-black and
credits. Outside, the freezing rain
has coated the trees with grey

and nothing moves
but drops like dribble sliding from a cold chin,
each twig encased in ice. *The end.*
I'll click the button, watch it through again.

Susan Wicks

Karen Aqua (animator) and Ken Field (composer): *Sensorium*

Woman and Alsatian

She seems just about to move
having agreed,
one hand comforts the dog,
buried into the fur behind his ears,
but he doesn't like my camera.

I saw them from across the street
and followed, attracted by
the slick pvc of her coat,
which gave her a beatnik look,
though practical too, I can see that.

Her dog lollops on oversized feet.
He will grow quickly,
they already work as a team.
What's his name?
I position them by a blank wall.

Look at me. They are both unsure.
She wonders why I am interested in her –
ordinary, out for a walk, hair a mess.
She half smiles, tense. *His name is Timber.*
The dog barks.

Rose Cook

Photograph: Keith Arnatt

104

The Hares of Birkenau

He loved hares
      remembering how
in Patagonia
the dash of one
across his path
had made him feel
      astonishingly alive
and how
when shooting scenes
at Birkenau
two hares
      bewildered at first
had skilfully contorted their way
through the dense barbed wire
as prisoners had failed to

They could also deceive death
      that greatest deceiver

He hoped his people
would choose to come back
as hares

Wendy Klein

Claude Lanzmann: *Shoah*

105

Seeing a Likeness

This very young man could be you,
my long-ago lover. He has your profile:
Roman nose, curved narrow lips,
thick eyebrows, unruly dark hair.
But here he's a German soldier, a prisoner
fixed in black and white, in Sicily, 1943.
He's wounded, afraid of death,
his eyes closed in pain.

A world of wars spins before the lens.
Capa steps on a mine and dies.
We focus down on coins in the hand.
You grow old in a distant place,
your soldiering done, your hair
the same – but a torrent of silver.

Jenny Morris

Photograph: Robert Capa

November 1918

This time the soldier is British,
on sentry duty, rifle in hand,
khaki battle-dress itching

and the girl is Italian,
leaning on the wall of sand-bags
where he can't help but see her.

She laughs and teases,
ignores her mother's warnings;
a film star disguised as a peasant.

He grins back at her –
whatever he was meant to be guarding
could shrivel to dust for all he cares.

And this time, a photographer was passing,
who caught in that glance
all those other days

when he was a Roman and she was an Angle
when he's a Yank and she's Vietnamese
when a moment is all that it takes.

Maggie Butt

William Joseph Brunell: *British sentry and Italian peasant woman*

Aperture

The sun sets a thousand times
In parallel arcs along 54th St.

Look closely –
Old structures are replaced by new,

A façade is rendered translucent,
Trees disappear.

In the horizontal drift of light
You will notice

That one hot summer night
His office window was left open.

You can just make out
Blurred outlines of human activity:

The subtle shifting of a lamp,
A coat draped over a chair,

Just long enough to register.
The details tell the story –

The dark shutter, the streetlight.
This is his one appearance.

Focus on the top-right corner –
His absence is clearly evident.

Deborah Sloan

Michael Wesely: *Open Shutter* at The Museum of Modern Art, New York 2004.

Maybe

River in spate
sun god behind clouds
one arch of Devil's Bridge still standing
a man, maybe, who fishes from that arch
black against the foaming river
arms high in supplication
held high, maybe, in desperation;
but the link from light to dark
from god to the devil
has gone
maybe in recent floods
maybe a hundred years before
maybe this is all there ever was.

Mary Chuck

Unattributed postcard: *Ponte Diavolo, near Lucca*

Hen Party

From high in the heated perfumed air
you catch the vibe – a whirl, a blur,
see shoulders – plump –
hear clucking tongues –
find tenderness in all that flesh.

Feet jig hands clutch,
gilt chains gleam on perky breasts,
bra straps, silver sandals, bling;
faces pink and damp with sweat
red lips nibbling chicken wings.

Up they get and round they spin,
twirling girls in gales of tulle,
a reek of perfume, stink of gin –
dancing their way to daylight in
the wheeze of smoke from cigarettes.

Seething prophecy of buds,
promises the yield to come,
laughter bursts from gaping mouths;
this is their season in the sun –
hear them cluck their harvest home.

Lindy Newns

Photograph: Rik Jundi

Into Silence

Afterwards I think how quietly he made
his brothers' habits, laying the fabric flat on a board
and pulling the selvedge straight, working quietly
in winter light with measuring tape and scissors,
moving unhurriedly from side to side
and folding, unrolling a bolt of cloth
and silently taking what he needed,
silently putting each unnecessary thing away.

How would it be to spend a life
endlessly pinning and tacking in a quiet room
as the sun moved slowly from one window to another
and shadows lengthened across the table,
to sew the long straight seam under the arms
and down each side, and along the centre of the hood,
hemming the heavy skirts by hand, the all-concealing sleeves?

It would be better without faith,
the room truly only a bare room
and nothing in it but cloth
and table, sunlight, scissors, pins and tape,
the steady slanting of time
as you sagged and stiffened, your body disgraced by age
like his, so that all the spaces that might have held belief

were open, empty, available,
echoing with height and winter,
the need to go on working quietly,
the need to love, to take care of the body.

Susan Wicks

Philip Gröning: *Le Grand Silence*

111

Inheritance

I carried the length to this room,
nailed to the table. It is paper.
It is art. You do not need me
to make the connection.

I painted it without ends,
recorded this borrowed table
with the papered edge
which is now yours.

Look at the rip, the dagger fold.
See the hammered metal
your hands can't remove.
A piece of nothing. Touch it.

Draw on it,
write your name.

Fiona Ritchie Walker

Unattributed photograph of a painter's studio

Snapshot

A creased snap of a mother, suitably dressed
stern-eyed, facing her daughter
who's leaning forward, hands clasped
behind her back, head lowered
to the concrete between them.

It's tricky to make out the fabric
of her slim calf-length suit. (Worsted perhaps.)
She's smirking like a guilty child –
toeing the line, her ill-at-ease expression
caught for anyone to see.

A sad exchange and not exactly Annie Leibovitz
but this shot tells me more in a split second
than I could learn about them in a lifetime.

Kerry Darbishire

Found in a saleroom suitcase

Birthday Girl

Your photograph at lovely twenty-one
gives me an image that speaks grace,
beauty, like the roses at your breast,
in full bloom. Never guessed that quarrel
with your sister! Nor ever knew your face
unmarked by time, your eyes so calmly blue,
unclouded by the knowledge of your future.
Your hair that ash blonde hue, thirties' waves
framing your fixed firm gaze.

My image is more shrouded, shadowed
by loving and losing you. Long years
a mother too, like you devoted
to her children, I search your black and white
for my past truth. Gazing down the telescope
of time, find mirrored in that image not myself,
but grandchildren, whose images you never knew.

Rosemary Doman

Portrait photograph from family archive

Note to My Son

I love the book of photographs you sent.
I like especially the portraits of Muhammad Ali,
Seamus Heaney and the famous one
of Beckett – Godot man. And others, unknowns,
feel to me uncannily familiar.
Two old dears, one short, one tall, one fat,
one thin, are wearing warm felt hats that hug
their heads. They're like my aunties Dorothy
and Madge. The men in flat caps at a pony
fair and the one who smokes a pipe and picks
up sticks remind me of my father.
And what is that untidy-haired, leather-
jacketed chap who taught me English Lit.
doing at a farmers' demonstration
in 1965?

I'm being fooled by fashions of the times.
But understanding that won't stop me
having more encounters with the dead:
a tourist from America holds up
a little camera. It's ready to be lifted
in an instant to her eager, focused eyes.
She is, for a few moments, my mother.
And a dark-haired youth in dark-framed specs
is just about to give up concentrating
on the engineering task he has
in hand to smile at me with your dad's
own smile beside a rural railway track
in Hampshire where I know he never was
in 1960.

Janet Loverseed

Jane Bown: *A Lifetime of Looking*

115

Apollo, 1968

They floated past the moon without a spark
of radio, the quiet before birth.
Pulsed by its cobalt seas, they watched the Earth
its perfect O, rise trustful from the dark

as we wish children might, without a mark.
See South America, whose tides of white
shield sloths, jewelled hummingbirds which drink our light.
I was too young, swirled into my own dark.

At work, in a Tech Library, an Ark
of students, I set blue Earth on the wall
so it sailed to them, bold and beautiful.
In drawers, the plans for windpower slept in dark.

The blue seas rose, then drowned. We lost the lark.
I never dreamed that we would reach such dark.

Alison Brackenbury

Based on the famous photograph of Earth taken from space

a tangle of magic carpets

Reading, After Dark

The city that isn't a city, not yet, is on a night out,
wearing its glitziest bling. The road is a dancefloor,
a double-view mirror that throws back the flicker
of streetlights, its dance to the jitter of tree-leaf
and shimmying branch.
                        Sat slap in the path
by the gas works, there's a wide-hatted man,
who's at furious work with fat brushes and dollops
of paint onto canvas-sized boards, his tealights
and Tilley lamp doing their thing in the dark
till it's lit up like Christmas.

The city that isn't, is shifting its edges in time
to the rhythm of colour, the jazz riff of brushstrokes
flung down by the man who's alight with himself,
whose heart syncopates to the hum of a city, the painter
whose brush makes it glow in the dark, makes it radiant.

Susan Utting

Ray Atkins' exhibition of paintings at Reading Museum's Madejski Gallery

Admiring the Still Lives

Light-headed, I walk through the spaces of the gallery
(they back away, don't like me). All those gold-
encrusted virgins and landscapes hang unimportant,
in one dimension. I smell only the food.

Brown loaves. Cool wine in the glittering decanter.
Redcurrants. Water melon, deep pure green.
Fish on its silver salver, a knife ready
to cut it. Only this field of air between.

The juices rise in my gorge; I'd like to
snatch, rip the canvas open. It's a day
and night since I've eaten. And the well-fed thousands
stare blind, float past me in the gallery.

Merryn Williams

At the Ashmolean Museum, Oxford

A Day at the Gallery

The child, painted for serious innocence,
like all such receptacles for our vagrant souls,
resonates an intense sadness, the burden of a life
seized, cut and bound – that gold mantle
clearly weighs her down – and what's with this
littering her with black goats? This whole set-up
has got my goat –
                                                    so,
while the peacocks and monkeys gather for milking,
a Queen Bee gives birth in the hive to a full-grown
Athene who will steal her crown; before Persephone
– who knows Pandora has opened her disdainful box
to every poisoned wanna-be in the world –
puts on the red stilettos and heads for town,
I'm pulling up this pink gerbera that has planted itself
in the dank surround of a bottomless wishing well
and turning this greenwood thinking around.
                                                    Child,
shuck off that golden mantle – it won't save us anyhow –
have those demobbed goats trample it into the ground.
Child, become human again. Leave now. Go wild.

Anne Stewart

From a variety of art postcards

Tales from the Sculpture Park

Who is this striding out of the forest
urgent and zealous with news
of a scoop? If he was human
he'd tread on the celandines –
if he was real, not rock.

I loop with a path
to the bluebell wood where a silver
carapace shines in the sun and two great boulders
are giants in love, so close
they almost could kiss.

Deeper in, it's cold:
the wolf has his sniper-eye fixed on a sheep,
a headless Ganesha approves.

This must be
where the Wild Hunt stopped
one blackthorn winter to set down its dead –

Yet there's spring in this clearing, a reason
for yellow and they are still here, these symbols,
these clues – clear as the sparrows
but hidden by leaves...

There are bulletins here for a man in a hurry
and ladders of glass to the sky.

Mandy Pannett

At the Cass Foundation, Goodwood

Meeting Apollo

Snide giggle of soft rain on foliage
As I recognised him in the garden.
Tenth statue among the damp shrubs. Apollo.
I shed tears in exchange for his wet blessing,
Apotheosis of a naughty whim.

There was a tangle of steel reinforcement
Beckoning from a lump of broken concrete
That somebody had chucked into a skip;
A lucky find, a nice bit of rough trade
Calling out, asking to be taken home.

Compassion for the beauty in found things
Gave me the right to take it; now it lives
Lovely in long grass in my own garden,
Moss on its plinth, rust on the twisted rods
That mimic the perfection of Apollo.

That's how I live, occasionally blessed
By random glimpses of the sad old god
Who wanders through the wreckage of the world
Twanging the slack strings of a busted lyre,
Seeking an echo in a mortal heart.

Ann Drysdale

At the Barbara Hepworth Sculpture Garden

Virtues of Unity

He seemed invisible to visitors,
though he was dressed in a costume
of the period, and his wig resembled
curved waves of a waterfall.

In truth, I thought he was part
of the installation: thirty-nine spheres,
each one representing a country and
made from the clay of this country.

He moved slowly anticlockwise,
stopped at the small ceramic vessel,
a creamy white called *Faith*.
The positive quality of Germany.

A slow smile grew on his face
when he saw there were no openings,
that the vessel seemed restful,
flowering into a solid cathedral.

Russet, tan, black, brown, beige, taupe,
grey, creamy-white, white. Eyes fixed
on his native country, he started humming
Jesu, joy of man's desiring, and I was glad.

Fokkina McDonnell

Halima Cassell: *Virtues of Unity*

The Matter of Size

All alone in the ship-shaped gallery
the architect dubbed the Fish, Serra
found a space for his mammoth snake to thrive.

To travel the curves of the snake's steel corridors
is to stroll through a medieval town,
the sky a mere ribbon of light.

But the Fish is dwarfed by the rest of the flagship,
Ghery's whale of a museum,
the city's metallic-white flower.

The inner petals of this titanium rose
shield the heart of the blossom,
its outer petals – Bilbao itself.

Snake in fish
Fish in ship
Ship in flower

Barbara Dordi

Richard Serra's *Snake* at the Guggenheim Museum, Bilbao

This Art

This art tells stories of a few known things
in black and white, of seals and walruses and bears
and caribou in ivory or rock; the close dark hives
of igloos; fish. A soapstone woman kneels,
her two white plaits escaping from her hood.

Here are the huntings and migrations,
kayaks and dog-teams and pack-sledges
carved out of stone or horn, and polished smooth
as if by ice. Here is the owl-man waiting, here's the wife
stretching her skins, the otter suckling, the two bears in rut.

The Inuit mother in her dark *aumak*
is a girl with two heads: her new-born child
grows from her shoulders. Everything she sees
her child sees too, each tiny carving cries
its uses. Every toothpick is a small harpoon.

Two seated figures hold their arms outstretched
from their muffled trunks, as if each contact hurts.
The cribbage boards are little ivory boats
with bears for figureheads, their intricate pale decks
pierced by ten dozen holes.

Susan Wicks

At the Museum of Inuit Art, Toronto

Island of Unlived Lives

Before the young man sees the island
its ring calls him out of the wood,
an airy sound like alpine grazing.
He's drawn toward migraine flashes.
Pulse rises. It's mesmerising,
a semaphore he can't decipher.

A boat floats half-way
between bank and lake-isle
moored to a buoy.
No oars. An invisible ferryman
will row him out
to the feathery limbs of that willow

Fearing what might wait there
he dithers like he's often done
swithering between
the sweet song
and the dim wood.
Turns back like before.

Anne Hay

Christian Boltanski:*Animitas*

The White Boat

The child's world
is born on a white boat

But these children have fixed on
dead birds and dead suns,
a papier-mâché babe wailing
and paper-trees
littered with old cartons,
cigarette-packs

everything documented
without magic or mercy:

their multiple-voice shrilling.

It spits in your eye
an anti-revolution
dropping warnings over plugged-up rivers
as a frilly lady smiles papery
out of the crumpled span of her hat

and the last white boat
sticks on a black canal.

Katherine Gallagher

Students 'Save Our Environment' exhibition 1971

Women's Arts Alliance Exhibition 1975

These kitchen utensils, wonky as bunioned feet,
hanging in an unruly gaggle on the wall, return me
to the musical beat of a wooden spoon canoodling
with batter, the swish of a fork mashing potatoes.

Let me praise women tied into aprons
in sweltering kitchens: mums, aunties, family friends,
making ends meet by concocting cheese on toast
from stale bread, and scraping out the last of the jam
to make a scattering of tarts with leftover pastry.

Know that we struck and shook and rattled your utensils
till their wood and metal clatter
ran down the stairs and through old-gent London streets
whose flat fronts were in need of a stitch and a polish.

Can you hear our blows, our hoo-hah,
as you lean towards two-bar electric fires,
knitting lumpy jumpers for girls who couldn't settle
at home like tabbies by the fire
but instead are prowling round London, caterwauling?

Caroline Gilfillan

Marion Lees-MacPherson's installation of kitchen utensils

Theatre

The sky was heating up
I could hardly breathe.

What with swallows
diving through it like kids in a pool,
all screaming.

What with the moon
ready to burst like a sack of water.

What with pavements
peeling themselves from earth,
hanging just above, just below,
a tangle of magic carpets.

What with people
fanning, spraying, drinking
slower and slower
until, work, what was that?

It seemed the sky was about to break
over every country in the world
where people gathered,

over palaces and chapels
made for popes, preachers,
prophets, saints,

for benediction, meditation, glory.

First the thunder a long way off
like a barrow wheeled over cobbles
around the corner,
a drum not played but rolled.

Next, cameras, matches,
the seam revealed.

Over savannahs sky played
like a boy striking a hammer
against metal dripping petrol.

Over the poles sky raged –
that they could be so cold,
that they could make shapes
sky never dreamed of,
that they could mimic earth.

Over cities sky was art.
It touched all there was on earth

the Algerian sweeping a courtyard,
the Malian digging a road,
the gardener from Poland,
her hands in the soil.

Jackie Wills

Production by Anatoli Vassiliev based on Pushkin's *Mozart and Salieri* using the music of Vladimir Martynov's *Requiem*. Festival d'Avignon 2006.

Under the Strobe

You are the shadows who have miniaturised the cryosphere
into a garden of paradise, yours the silhouettes facing fire.

Yours the skeletons, crystal wasps in the long black coffin,
spiders with eggsacs and glass intestines, stalagmites, goblins,

vertebrae and antlers, melting candles, yours the serpents
swallowing mice; infinite, interminable, your Lazarus dance.

Have you seen aerial fossils, spiculae, birdwings frozen in flight?
Kittens iced to branches, glazed drops, objects crystallised by light?

Yours the glass apple, glass core, that ballooning missing bite;
the wedding arch of crossed swords, apertures jagged as kites.

Go home and imagine them, you can't. Even as they're here,
now, they're gone. And everything outdoors, buildings by the river,

boats, buses on the bridge, everything that runs in lines will run
into fountain, the beauty of the arc against the formality of line.

Yours this catwalk, ghastly, spectacular, and all the faery forms
of fungus, plankton, Venus's girdle, that have swum through time.

Mimi Khalvati

Olafur Oliasson at the Hayward Gallery 2013

Shattered
the moon lies broken
sharp shapes and edges
wedged against overlapping
fragments junctions touching
the sky in ruins yet a lunar glow
spreads over random slivers of
space spread to four corners
of the universe men labour
to rebuild the planet
piece by piece

Barbara Hickson

Andy Goldsworthy: *Slate scratched on slate*

Bowl of Rice

Here is a bowl of rice –
for this your mother summons clouds
and disperses them.

She diverts rivers into each day of your life.
Birds sing for her in waterfields
drawing grain from stalk and leaves.
Mountains lend her echoes,
the snow from their peaks.

Her spoon serves a blessing of turmeric
to every lover you'll know.
With it come bellows, a clink of charcoal,
fingers spread like rakes
through midnight's shared groan.

Here is a bowl of rice –
for this your mother summons clouds
and disperses them.

Jackie Wills

The 'Rice Pavilion' exhibition 2007

Cappella Catharinae in Visby Cathedral

Even the deaf would hear
this music, its steady afternote
released years later, buzzing in the stone's throat.

Each vowel prolongs itself
in every pillar, each vibrating arch;
this place insists our voices are provisional.

However clear and crisp
we write our human music, this
discordant echo is the cathedral's voice.

The singing rises, builds
and shivers, hangs in a trapped chord
that stings our ear-drums, swelling behind the words.

Susan Wicks

At St Mary's Cathedral, Gotland

that we make such things

Marking the Years

It hung from the mantle tree, belt or door in the northern lands
where moor, lake and forest were tamed.
Rough hands took wood to fashion it, square it, a cubit's length,
made a moon ruler of months, weeks, days;
marking time to turn furrow, plant, lie fallow.
For the watcher in the night, silvered by waxing and waning light,
there was no adjustment of quarter days
– he hooked his year to the moon.
Wise as a beast, he followed the plough across the winter skies.
On its four sides, one for each season, he carved his runes
obedient to his church, the festivals and fasts remembered by
a saint's shoes, a love knot; a cross, a sword, an axe.
He called them his Moon Ruler, Rimstock or Primestave.
These smooth stafas, shaped the name of a place that
took root, leaved and flowered.

Liz Parkes

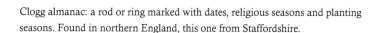

Clogg almanac: a rod or ring marked with dates, religious seasons and planting
seasons. Found in northern England, this one from Staffordshire.

Herm

It would have been too heavy
for Ton alone to carry to his front door.
It looks like wood but it's the colour of unfired clay,
pebbles half-embedded, its twirls and twists suggesting

mud, no, limestone, or bone, yes, bone,
the thigh of a great beast, I could go and find the head,
eye-sockets, teeth, its claws, its carcass polished, leathery,
a Mummy case, a replica maybe by Ton himself

who never found it except inside his head,
carved it in bleached almond wood to make a totem
with bores and boles, grazes, cuts
where ants can run and insects lodge and breed

and house their grubs, for bugs mean birds
and Ton loves birds: you can hear them now, a turtle dove,
bee-eater, oriole and so of course that's why it's here
leaning upright by his front door.

Hilary Elfick

Ton Out's doorpost at La Masia dels Artistes

The Foramina of Saint Osmund

I am Stone.
Place your hands
in the arched hollows of the tomb
palms down. Place your forehead there
your face, any broken parts of your body
or perhaps your broken mind,
I can wait while you touch
each ridge, scratch and indent
until your skin cannot feel
where you end and I begin.

My heaviness reaches down
to where the falling stops
the ground gasps.
Songs rest here
I am quiet.
Shall I begin the work
of listening into your stillness
as it echoes through me
like a bell ?

I am Saint Osmund's Stone
I breathe out the impress
of a saint, I dissolve
into your hushed whispers,
come place your hands
near the singing bones
and let your darkness
melt into prayer.

Hilary Stobbs

The Foramina shrine was a means of prayer whereby the supplicant could feel close to the relics of the saint. The shrine had 'portholes' cut into the sides and the supplicant's head, arms, legs or upper body could be inserted into the apertures for healing.

Stained Glass Statements

Here, I think, a young man (though not young when I encountered him)
sat through compulsory chapel, termtime Sunday after Sunday
while others yawned or dozed, but however boring
or interesting the sermon, it would have been impossible
to take his eyes off those windows. Abraham, a Dutchman,
had painted these extraordinary scenes circa 1631.
How did they escape? Perhaps the college,
rich enough to pay for them, was secluded
enough for the smashers of sacred glass to go elsewhere.
Awe-inspiring visions, huge expanses of water,
furious clouds, the whale heaving up to devour Jonah,
Judgment Day, Christ seated on a rainbow, the naked
dead climbing up, the damned going down to everlasting fire.
The words went over his head, he dreamed of the seventeenth century,
rain and sun on the glass obscured or emblazoned the colours.
Oh, yes, he thought, one day I'm going to write about this.

Merryn Williams

Chapel windows in Queen's College, Oxford

Parable of the Sower

The wonder is
that they exist at all:
kingfisher and leaping trout,
hummingbird hawk moth
and pipistrelle bat,
the swallow and the swift,
purple loosestrife
and spiked star of Bethlehem,
this amber fox nosing
through brambles
who burns so brightly
when the sun shines through;
and the wonder is
that we make such things
as this stained glass window
where nothing chokes or withers,
nothing fails to thrive,
not the towering elm
or the partridges pecking
in the dirt, not the field poppy
or the dragonfly –
these few timely reminders
of all we stand to lose.

Ruth Sharman

Andrew Taylor: Chapel window at Great Chalfield

Refurbishment

Out of town to view some painterly seascapes:
the building's closed. We trudge back hot
for art: the galleries are bare. White space
has blanked out carpets, silver, jewels.
Nothing for it but next door: the disappointing
living dead, the dusty glass, the ponderous lofting
of a dinosaur.

Then in the gloom of ending day
a sudden bolt of blue. We peer, heads close
and see the whole of this lost afternoon
restored to glory in a tiny triptych.
Lapis, gold-festooned. Italianate,
sun-dowered, but displayed beside the battered wood
of an abused Madonna – English, circa 1300.

So it's ours. Each quiet country church
so plain and unassuming, spare and light
showed once like this. Such gilded glories
illuminated village lives, till a king's whim
eclipsed the sun. Bruised saints, white-plastered walls
are our inheritance: a cleansing force.

With brilliant capability of being
hidden in a pocket, held in the protecting curve
of a handspan, this small splendour has survived
the smash and grab of centuries. We have not.
Our sensibilities have been limewashed away
until a taste for purity, clean lines, clear spaces
pared down vision, has replaced as though god-given
the ecstacy of colour and the dream of faith.

Joy Howard

At the V&A, South Kensington

144

Tunc

The island monks knew exile,
the obduracy of stone,
the fickleness of wind and water.
They relished creaturely absurdity,
tracked wild colourings,
caught them in ink's alchemy,
learned that meaning is precious
as breath and as ephemeral, that
a book can be burned or plundered.

They wagered all on words,
words that could tell a tale to hold
the world in place, bind up
the disparate, words to be
wooed, adorned, subverted,
deft words like 'then' *tunc*
– hook between one crucifixion
and two others, between
two robbers and a derelict king –

its initial, a coiled cat feasting
on interlace of spook-eyed eels,
a spell cast between worlds
to lure the traveller's gaze.

Andrea Ward

The Book of Kells (folio 124r)

The Kilim

It was the cinnamon
turquoise
burnt orange groves
and saffron borders
that called me
into a garden
where birds perched
in tamarinds
and jasmine
wove pure threads of incense
took my breath
singing
to a river
soft under my feet
ancient speak
a language I knew
the way whales sound
swallows migrate
wild geese trace landmarks
the way leaves fall
earth stills
moon waxes
tides swell
and stars
pattern a night sky
lead nomads to pasture

Kerry Darbishire

In a carpet seller's shop, Paphos

Jade Horse

Han dynasty horse
of dappled aquamarine,
survivor of long centuries
in cool jade segments,
gleaming torso twisting
through cabinet glass,
stone nostrils flared
to test the gallery air,
ears peaked and pointing in
above a glistening brow
and chiselled eyes.

> The clean-cut mane is chipped,
> your broad chest muscle-tensed,
> your firm mouth open to neigh
> a triumphant challenge down
> your sea-horse-elongated nose,
> your noble head ready to soar
> as you rear on absent legs,
> your potent quarters vanished
> in a Chinese whisper,
> and dragon wings perhaps
> or coiled sea creature's tail...

> Precious horse from a green past,
> astride you, we ride beyond
> our petty present
> into waves of foam-flecked
> dappled dreams.

Debjani Chatterjee

Torso from the 'Precious' exhibition at Sheffield's Millennium Galleries

Anonymous

Spray-paint on the concrete gun-emplacement.
Where does it come from, this urge to decorate?
Galloping straight from the cave wall, so deep

That light cannot reach it. The effigy's magic.
The Instagram to say, I was here. But here, where the gulls
Settle and lift, to stumble across four

Willow-woven brent geese, caught in mid-flight
Near the hide at the Lough's edge, and know
Nothing about their maker,

Seems entirely right: as if
They have risen straight from water and soil
Where they have lain for thousands of years, like the lost skill

Of naming something precisely, without words.

Katrina Porteous

On Holy Island, Northumberland

Two Worlds

Magnetised by light, gulls are caught
in this circular glass building –
but the gulls fly on my right-hand side,
scooping the river's path,
it's only their duplicates mirrored
in the curving windows on my left.

In this shining field of glass,
Williams Car Sales is reflected,
large and clear.
(I could buy two cars the same,
one of them virtual.)

Waiting at the red light here
I find myself in that unlikely place,
two worlds at once,
driving apparently in sky, with gulls,
and passing the Williams show-room
on both sides.

Gill McEvoy

On Dock Road, Liverpool

The Art of Folding

It has taken her years
to perfect the art of folding
herself small enough
to fit inside her own palm.
See how she lowers her eyes
to become an offering.
Even her shadow has gone.

No-one will miss her
until they are hungry.

All they will find
is a sprinkling of cardamom,
scent of cinnamon,
something familiar
in the angle and curve
of the wooden spoon
resting on her kitchen table.

Fiona Ritchie Walker

Magazine feature about the art of folding napkins.

Tea for Two

Tea for two. Not a thirties set piece,
rose patterned china, little finger raised
above elegant grip, velvety slip
from a gilded rim, imprinting half
a kiss. Intimate twosome, gossip
duet, played over cucumber bites,
dainty iced nibbles, silvery percussion
of spoon against cup. The doily ritual.

Here, harmony is in stubby spouts,
wedge handles, lollipop colours. Blue
balloon trees on trunks of brown scribble
twist mischievously to base. Jug, bowl,
beat loudly in tune, open purse mouths
shouting their designer's mind. No coy,
sweet glances slyly passed with the sugar!

Dizzying saucers and spinning top plates
dare you to rest a crustless cress sandwich.
Burslem's bold Art Deco queen
takes on the teaset, a signature piece.

Rosemary Doman

Clarice Cliff teaset

151

Library

Light is the first thing –
how it pools and flows from windows
spread like sheets to catch its slightest stir.

Space is the next, the way
the walls, paced by the galleries
and shelves, lift to a new dimension.

Form orders each strong shaft
and beam to fuse the strength of wood
with ribcage rhythm.

Time's pendulum swings back from here
to creaking galleons, cathedral choirs,
forward to the Bauhaus and beyond.

Jean Watkins

Glasgow School of Art

A Measure of Stillness

Through yellowed wheat, sunflowers
along straight roads sparse with trees,
summer's haze shearing the air,
suddenly rising above the plain,
the non-identical spires.

As I drive closer,
the cathedral seems to disappear
among tower-blocks,
factories, streets zigzagging
around mediaeval hills –

this pilgrimage to Chartres
where I am learning
to take my cue
from its heart –
its dance in space –

and never to take my eyes
from the spires, the bowl,
the ark lifting
burning
into a teal sky.

Katherine Gallagher

In the Loire Valley

source of the blaze

Refraction

If I were to paint it
you'd never know
where to find it,
that source
of the blaze
on Cézanne's apples.
that wisp on the neck
of Vulliard's sewing woman,
the deep shine of faith
in the face
of Old Woman Reading,
or the wink, lurking in the folds
of Rembrandt's bulbous nose.

If you look
you can find it in music,
on the bald head of a baby,
in the curve of hands touching
and even in the shadow
they make on the road.

When the last pheasant
is shot
and the sludge settles in the massive oil tanks
waiting for nobody,
when the last tree falls from the memory
of no-one,
it will still be there,
skittering, pottering,
reflecting.

Kate Foley

The Poets

Sheila Aldous is widely published in journals and webzines and has won or been placed in several competitions. Recent publications include a chapbook, *Patterns Of All Made Things* (Hen Run), and *Paper Boats: The Burning of Teignmouth and Shaldon 1690* (Indigo Dreams).

Moniza Alvi was born in Lahore. Three of her collections *The Country at My Shoulder* (OUP, 1993), *Europa* (Bloodaxe, 2008) and *At the Time of Partition* (Bloodaxe, 2013), have been shortlisted for the TS Eliot Prize.

Penny Ayers lives in Cheltenham. She has won prizes in competitions including the Cardiff International Poetry Competition 2013 and has been published in *Brittle Star, The Dawntreader* and *ArtemisPoetry*. She helps run the Gloucestershire Writers' Network.

Denise Bennett is widely published and has an MA in creative writing. She runs poetry workshops in community settings and has published three collections – *Planting the Snow Queen* and *Parachute Silk* (Oversteps Books) and *Water Chits* (Indigo Dreams).

Sara Boyes has three collections: *Kite* (Stride, 1989), *Wild Flowers* (Stride, 1993) and *Black Flame*, a pamphlet (Hearing Eye, 2005). She's been an actor, a playwright and, for many years, a tutor in creative writing.

Alison Brackenbury was born in 1953. Her work has won Eric Gregory and Cholmondeley Awards, and has frequently been broadcast on BBC Radio. *Gallop*, her 2019 Selected Poems, is published by Carcanet. New poems can be read on her website.

Carole Bromley is a York-based poet. She has three collections from Smith/Doorstop, a pamphlet, *Sodium 136,* with Calder Valley and a collection, *The Peregrine Falcons of York Minster,* forthcoming from Valley Press.

Maggie Butt lives in London. Her fifth poetry collection is *Degrees of Twilight* (The London Magazine, 2015). A novel *The Prisoner's Wife* was published by Penguin imprints in the UK and USA in spring 2020 under the name Maggie Brookes.

Debjani Chatterjee is an award-winning poet, translator and arts therapist. Her seventy books include *The Elephant-Headed God & Other Hindu Tales*, a Children's Book of the Year, and six poetry collections. Honours include Sheffield Hallam University's honorary doctorate and RLF Fellowships.

Alison Chisholm is a poetry tutor and adjudicator, and the author of twelve collections. She writes poetry columns for *Writing Magazine*, and textbooks on the craft of writing poetry.

Mary Chuck began writing poetry when she retired having listened to wonderful poetry at the Wordsworth Trust, where she is a Trustee. She writes in Grasmere, Cumbria, Warrington, and on residential courses. She is also a Primary School Governor.

A C Clarke was a winner in the Cinnamon 2017 pamphlet competition with *War Baby*. Her fifth collection is *A Troubling Woman* (Oversteps Books) and a collaborative pamphlet *Drochaid*, was published last year. She is working on poems about Gala Éluard/Dalí.

Gillian Clarke holds the Queen's Gold medal for Poetry 2010 and the Wilfred Owen Award 2012. Her *Selected Poems* is from Picador and a tenth collection, *Zoology*, from Carcanet. Her version of the 7th century Welsh poem *Y Gododdin* will appear from Faber in 2021.

Chris Considine now lives in Devon, having left Yorkshire. Her fifth collection, *Seeing Eye*, was published by Cinnamon Press in 2019.

Rose Cook is a poet and photographer who lives in Devon. She co-founded the popular Devon poetry and performance forum *One Night Stanza,* as well as poetry performance group *Dangerous Cardigans*. She has four collections, and a Hen Run chapbook *Sightings* (2019).

Pamela Coren lives in Sedbergh, and is retired from teaching English at the University of Leicester. She's published academic papers and many poems. Her first collection was *The Blackbird Inspector*. A second, *Shaving the Bell,* is on its way in 2021.

Doris Corti writes under her maiden name, and is published in poetry magazines, collections and anthologies. A nonagenarian, her mini memoir is *Muffins for Tea*. She is a regular contributor to *Writing Magazine*, leads a U3A poetry group and is vice president of the Society of Women Writers and Journalists (SWWJ).

Kerry Darbishire lives in Cumbria where her poetry is rooted. She has two poetry collections published by Indigo Dreams and is working on a third. Her poems have won several prizes and have appeared widely in magazines and anthologies.

Kelly Davis was born in London and lives in Maryport, West Cumbria, where she works as a freelance editor. Her poems have been published in magazines (including *Mslexia* and *The Journal*) and in Arachne, Handstand and Grey Hen Press anthologies.

Julia Deakin is West Yorkshire-based and a keen walker, birder and ice skater. Widely published, each of her four collections won praise from leading UK poets. She edits *Pennine Platform* magazine, and has won many prizes – none of them for skating.

Rosemary Doman is a former English/Creative writing tutor and long term poet. An occasional prize winner, her poems have been published in a number of anthologies. An exhibition at her local Walker Art Gallery was among prompts for poems published here.

Barbara Dordi edits *The French Literary Review,* a bilingual arts magazine. She is working on a second collection of English poems, after twelve years in France where she published several chapbooks, two books of bilingual poetry, and a biography of the Impressionist Achille Laugé.

Ann Drysdale has published seven poetry collections, as well as memoir, essays and a gonzo guidebook to the City of Newport. She lives in the topmost terrace of a mining town in South Wales.

Anne Eccleshall dabbled with writing poetry for years but in 2012 took the plunge and began studying at the Poetry School. She has recently moved to Norfolk and now finds that wide skies and hedgerow birds often feature in her poems.

Hilary Elfick is an experienced broadcaster who has published over twenty five books. She has travelled through almost fifty countries, both writing and performing. The natural world features in most of her work, which has been particularly studied by postgraduate students in London and Bucharest.

Kate Foley has ten collections, the most recent published by Arachne Press in 2018. Her last day job was Head of English Heritage's research laboratories. Her poems have all been published post-retirement. She is currently president of the Suffolk Poetry Society.

Katherine Gallagher is London-based and Australian-born. A keen environmentalist, she has six full collections. Her most recent are *Acres of Light* (Arc Publications, 2016) and *Carnival-Edge: New & Selected Poems,* Arc Publications, 2010). Her poems are widely-published in the UK and Australia

Rebecca Gethin has written five poetry publications and has been a Hawthornden Fellow and a Poetry School tutor. *Messages* was a winner in the first Coast to Coast to Coast pamphlet competition. Her latest collection *Vanishings* has just been published by Palewell Press.

Caroline Gilfillan is the author of five poetry collections, one of which, *Yes*, won the East Anglian Book Award for the best poetry collection. In 2019 she won the Yeovil Prize for Poetry. www.carolinegilfillan.co.uk

Susanna Harding is a writer, theatre practitioner and festival director. Her poetry has been published in several journals and anthologies, including *Grey Hen Press, The North, Equinox, Orbis, Smiths Knoll, Dreamcatcher, New Walk, The Frogmore Papers, Obsessed with Pipework,* and *Stand.*

Pauline Hawkesworth is published in anthologies and magazines and has four publications: from Mitre Press, and from Redbeck, IDP 2007 and IDP pamphlet competitions. She was an athletics coach and administrator for fifty years and is President of the Portsmouth Poetry Society

Anne Hay lives in Edinburgh. Her poems have been published in anthologies and magazines including *Magma, Gutter, Envoi* and *Northwords Now*. She was a winner of the Scottish Book Trust New Writers' Award 2020.

Barbara Hickson has twelve poems published in a shared collection *Rugged Rocks, Running Rascals* (DragonSpawn Press, 2019). Her poems have appeared in magazines, anthologies and on-line journals, and been placed in several competitions including Magma and The Plough Prize.

Doreen Hinchliffe is originally from Yorkshire and now lives in South East London. She has published two poetry collections – *Dark Italics* (Indigo Dreams) and *Substantial Ghosts* (Oversteps Books). Her first novel *Sarabande in Blue* was recently published by Blossom Spring Publishing.

Joy Howard has been running Grey Hen Press since 2007. She relocated to Cumbria from W Yorks in 2015 to be closer to family and do the recommended downsizing – a task hampered by ongoing magpie tendencies and piles of new books.

Nora Hughes grew up in Belfast and now lives in London. Her poems have appeared in a number of poetry magazines and anthologies. Her pamphlet *Under Divis Mountain* won the Templar 2020 iOTA Shot Award.

Rosie Jackson is widely published. Her awards include 1st Poetry Space 2019, 1st Wells 2018, 1st Stanley Spencer 2017. Her latest collection, with Graham Burchell, is *Two Girls and a Beehive: Poems about Stanley Spencer and Hilda Carline* (Two Rivers Press, 2020).

Maria Jastrzębska is a poet, editor and translator. Her most recent collection is *The True Story of Cowboy Hat and Ingénue* (Cinnamon Press, 2018). *The Cedars of Walpole Park,* her selected poems, were translated into Polish (Stowarzyszenie Żywych Poetów, 2015).

Mimi Khalvati has published nine collections with Carcanet Press. Her most recent is *Afterwardness*, a PBS Wild Card and book of the year in *The Sunday Times* and *The Guardian*. She is a Fellow of the Royal Society of Literature.

Angela Kirby was born in rural Lancashire in 1932 and now lives in London. Her poems have appeared in many magazines and anthologies, and have won prizes and commendations in several major competitions. Shoestring Press has published her five collections.

Wendy Klein has four collections, the most recent *Into the Blue, Selected Poems* (High Window Press, 2019). Her pamphlet *Let Battle Commence*, based on her great-grandfather's letters home as a Confederate Soldier in the American Civil War, was recently launched on radio.

Thelma Laycock lives in Leeds. She has two poetry collections published by Indigo Dreams Publishing and a collection of interlinked short stories published by Stairwell Books.Some of her work has been translated into Hebrew, Romanian, Italian, French and Welsh.

Gill Learner has won a number of prizes, been published in many magazines, and in anthologies including several from Grey Hen Press. She has two collections from Two Rivers Press, Reading, with a third due in 2021. More at www.poetrypf.co.uk.

Janet Loverseed is a retired teacher. Her pamphlet, *The Under-Ripe Banana*, was published by HappenStance, and a full collection, *The Shadow Shop*, published by Oversteps Books. A new collection, *Ježibaba,* is expected from Dempsey & Windle in October 2020.

Mandy Macdonald lives in Aberdeen, making poetry and music. Her work appears in several Grey Hen publications and in many anthologies and journals in print and online, and her debut pamphlet *The Temperature of Blue* (www.bluesalt.co.uk) appeared in early 2020.

Fokkina McDonnell has three collections: *Another life* (Oversteps Books, 2016), *Nothing serious, nothing dangerous* (Indigo Dreams, 2019) and the pamphlet *A Stolen Hour* (Hen Run, 2020). She received a Northern Writers Award 2020 from New Writing North.

Gill McEvoy lives in Devon and was a 2012 Hawthornden Fellow. She won the 2015 Michael Marks Award with *The First Telling* (Happenstance) and has two collections from Cinnamon Press: *The Plucking Shed* 2010 and *Rise* 2013. *Are You Listening?* is forthcoming from Hedgehog Press.

Rosemary McLeish sadly died shortly before the publication of this book. A Glasgow-born prize-winning poet and Outsider artist, she has been published widely in journals and anthologies, both poetry and prose. She has two collections of poetry published by Wordsmithery.

Jane Monach worked in mental health, education and psychotherapy. She lives in Sheffield where she writes and explores poetry with several groups.

Jenny Morris has five collections: *Urban Space, The Sin Eater, Lunatic Moon, Somnambulist* and *Domestic Damage.* She sees life sideways and writes about strange relationships.

Cheryl Moskowitz is a poet, novelist and creative translator. She writes for children and adults. She has published two collections and a novel. Her poetry has won many awards and can be found in several literary magazines in the UK and the US.

Frances Nagle is trying to fill the shocking holes in her reading and understanding of the classics as well as engaging with new and diverse fiction. And she's learning to play the concertina.

Lindy Newns has been shortlisted for several playwriting awards and poetry competitions and has won the Fresher prize for poetry. Her poetry and flash fiction has appeared in *Orbis, Riggwelter, L'Ephemère, Popshot* and the *Gaia* and *Poems for Grenfell* anthologies.

Jennie Osborne co-organises Teignmouth Poetry Festival. She has two collections, *How to be Naked* and *Colouring Outside the Lines,* and is working on a third, addressing our relationship with 'the other'. She has won the Kent and Sussex Poetry Competition and Ware Sonnet Prize.

Ness Owen is a poet and FE lecturer from Ynys Môn (Anglesey). Her poems and short stories have been widely published in journals and anthologies. Her first collection *Mamiaith* (Mother Tongue) was published by Arachne Press in 2019.

Mandy Pannett works freelance as a creative writing teacher. She is the author of four poetry collections, a pamphlet in English and Romanian parallel texts and two novellas. A new poetry collection will be published in the autumn 2020 by KFS Press.

Liz Parkes lives in Stourbridge, West Midlands. A former teacher, she belongs to several local poetry groups. She has been published in *Cannon's Mouth* and anthologies including *Unite Union* and three by Offa's Press.

Jo Peters has been published in magazines and anthologies and has had success in a number of competitions. Her pamphlet *Play* and her collection *Like yellow like flying* are published by Half Moon Books, Otley. When not writing she is reading, gardening, looking for wild flowers and spending the kids' inheritance.

Katrina Porteous is a Northumberland poet who often works in collaboration with other artists. She created *Horse* and three planetarium pieces with electronic composer Peter Zinovieff. Her collections from Bloodaxe include *The Lost Music* (1996), *Two Countries* (2014) and *Edge* (2019).

Jenny Pritchard has a teaching qualification in English, Speech and Drama and worked in primary education while raising a family. In 2014 she gained an MA in Fine Art. Poetry, a lifelong interest, is often referenced in her art.

Marka Rifat lives in Aberdeenshire and writes stories, poems and plays. This year, her work was selected by Grey Hen Press, *Lines+Stars*, *Northwords Now*, *Twisted Vine*, Lockdown Lore, the *San Joaquin Review*, *Rattle*, *GreenPrints* and Tangletree.

Elisabeth Rowe lives on Dartmoor and continues to write both serious and comic poetry. Her fourth collection *Timewise* was published by Oversteps Books in 2019. A collection of her comic verse *Diversion Ahead* is available from the author.

Hermione Sandall has been a drama teacher and, with her husband, a long distance sailor. She lives in Shropshire, and loves music and poetry.

Verity Schanche lives in Penzance and has been writing poetry for about fifteen years. Her poems have appeared in *South, Loose Muse, Dawn Treader* and *For The Silent*, an anthology to aid the work of The League Against Cruel Sports.

Ruth Sharman is a freelance translator specialising in French. She lives in Bath and has published two collections – *Birth of the Owl Butterflies* (Picador) and *Scarlet Tiger* (Templar) – and is working on a third focusing on India and the search for her roots.

Pat Simmons spent most of her working life as a copywriter for Oxfam, producing leaflets, appeal letters and books. She started writing poetry with commitment when she retired, and has appeared in several anthologies (including Grey Hen) and magazines.

Deborah Sloan is a Scot living in Sussex. She is a retired counsellor and now runs poetry therapy workshops with various groups including people living with dementia, recovering from addiction or struggling to come to terms with loss.

Anne Stewart has two full collections, the most recent being *The Last Parent* (SLP) and two small bi-lingual collections. She has won the Bridport Prize, Southport Poetry Prize and Poetry on the Lake's 'Silver Wyvern' (Italy). She created and runs www.poetrypf.co.uk.

Hilary Stobbs is an Aberdeen based poet whose work has appeared in various anthologies and periodicals. She won the Grey Hen chapbook competition 2015 with *Until It Rains* (Hen Run 2015). Her first full collection *Caught on the Inbreath* is due out from RGU in 2020.

Janet Sutherland has four poetry collections, most recently *Home Farm* (Shearsman Books, 2019) and is working on her fifth. Her poems are widely anthologised and published in magazines such as *Poetry Ireland Review, New Statesman* and *The Spectator*.

Susan Utting has poems published in *The Times, TLS, Forward Book of Poetry, Poetry Review, Poems on the Underground,* and broadcast at London's South Bank Centre for Poetry International. Her latest collection is *Half the Human Race: New & Selected Poems,*(Two Rivers Press).

Eleanor J Vale lives in Suffolk and her poems have been published in both magazines and anthologies. Her pamphlet *Think of Something Else* was published by The Garlic Press in 2016. She won the Grey Hen Poetry Competition in 2019.

Fiona Ritchie Walker grew up in a family of artists and spent her school years being told 'it's hard to believe you're Syd Walker's daughter'. Her father told her 'you paint in words' and she's been writing poetry and short fiction ever since.

Josie Walsh lives in Wakefield, where her commissioned poem is illustrated in ceramic tiles. Published in anthologies and magazines, she has read on radio and at festivals from her three collections: *Breathing Space* (2004), *Another Breath* (2009)and *Breathing Sky* (2018)

Andrea Ward is from Dublin and a teacher by profession. Her poetry has been published in Hennessy New Irish Writing (*The Irish Times*), *The Honest Ulsterman, Poetry Ireland Review, Skylight 47, Crannóg, Cyphers*, and the environmentalist magazine, *Channel*.

Jean Watkins lives near Reading. Her poems have appeared in many anthologies and magazines. Two Rivers Press published her first collection *Scrimshaw* in 2013 and the second, *Precarious Lives* in 2018.

Susan Wicks has eight collections, the most recent *Dear Crane* (Bloodaxe, 2021). Her work as poet and translator has won a number of awards. One of her three novels, *The Key* (Faber, 1997) was serialised on BBC's *Woman's Hour*. She lives in Kent.

Merryn Williams has five collections. Her latest is *The Fragile Bridge: New and Selected Poems'* (Shoestring Press). She is collecting poems for an anthology about the 2020 pandemic.

Jackie Wills has been a writer for more than forty years, working as a journalist, writing tutor and running reading groups.She's published six collections of poetry, her most recent is *A Friable Earth* (Arc, 2019).

Acknowledgements

SHEILA ALDOUS 'Age' previously published as 'The Light in Rembrandt's Mother' in *Acumen*. MONIZA ALVI 'Night Music' previously published as 'Eine Kleine Nachtmusik' *Split World: Poems 1990-2005* (Bloodaxe Books 2008). CAROLE BROMLEY 'Snow' *Ten Poems about Snow* (Candlestick Press 2019). MAGGIE BUTT 'Camera Obscura' published in *Under the Radar*. 'November 1918' published in *Orbis*. DEBJANI CHATTERJEE 'Jade Horse' previously published in a different version in *Jade Horse Torso: Poems and Translations* (Sixties Press, 2003). ALISON CHISHOLM 'Set in Stone' previously published as 'Pietà' *Hold Tight* (Headland Publications 2009). A C CLARKE 'Clydeside' published in *The Darg* (The Poets' Republic 2019). GILLIAN CLARKE 'Bach at St Davids' *A Recipe for Water* (Carcanet 2009). CHRIS CONSIDINE. 'Through Her Eyes' *Behind the Lines* (Cinnamon Press, 2011). ROSE COOK 'Woman and Alsatian' *Hearth* (Cultured Llama Publishing 2017). PAMELA COREN 'Tonus Peregrinus in Notre Dame' published in *Other Poetry*. KERRY DARBISHIRE 'The Kilim' *Distance Sweet on my Tongue* (Indigo Dreams 2018). BARBARA DORDI 'The Matter of Size' previously published as 'A Matter of Size' in *Aesthetica Creative Works Annual* 2011. ANN DRYSDALE 'Meeting Apollo' *Between Dryden and Duffy* (Peterloo 2005) and *Turn* (Exot Books 2013). HILARY ELFICK 'Herm' *This Is What Happens* (Hen Run 2019). KATHERINE GALLAGHER 'The White Boat' *Carnival Edge: New & Selected Poems* (Arc Publications 2010) and published in *Integral*; 'A Measure of Stillness' *Acres of Light* (Arc Publications, 2016). DOREEN HINCHLIFFE 'The Yearly Trick' *Substantial Ghosts* (Oversteps Books 2020). BARBARA HICKSON 'Under a Beech at Brantwood' previously published as 'Sitting under a Beech Tree at Brantwood' in *Living Words* (Swarthmoor Hall Press 2015). JOY HOWARD 'At the Window, Waiting' *Foraging (*Arachne Press 2016); 'Concerto', 'Refurbishment' and 'Old Crow' *Refurbishment* (Ward Wood Publications 2011); 'Song Without Words' previously published as 'Listening to Shostakovich' *Refurbishment* (Ward Wood Publications 2011). ROSIE JACKSON 'Homecoming' previously published as 'Resurrection' and 'Recovery Stroke' *The Light Box* (Cultured Llama 2016). MARIA JASTRZĘBSKA 'Everybody looks...' *The True Story of Cowboy Hat and Ingénue* (Liquorice Fish/Cinnamon Press 2018). MIMI KHALVATI 'Under the Strobe' previously published as 'Model for a Timeless Garden'*The Weather Wheel* (Carcanet 2014). ANGELA KIRBY 'Sad Litany' previously published as 'Design' in *Acumen*. THELMA LAYCOCK 'Rose' *A Difference in Direction* (Indigo Dreams Publishing 2015). GILL McEVOY 'Head Full of Birds' and 'Two Worlds' published in *Brittle Star*. CHERYL MOSKOWITZ 'Making Our Own Garden' *Poems for the Planet* with Julian Bishop, Maggie Butt and Sarah Doyle (Avington Books 2020). JENNIE OSBORNE 'Ambush' *Colouring Outside the Lines* (Oversteps Books 2015). MANDY PANNETT 'Tales from the Sculpture Park' published in *Agenda*. LIZ PARKES 'Marking the Year' previously published as 'Staffordshire Clogg Almanac'*The Poetry of Staffordshire* (Offa's Press 2015). JO PETERS 'Appearances' *Like yellow like flying* (Half Moon Books 2019). KATRINA PORTEOUS 'Anonymous' *Many Hands* (Peregrini Lindisfarne Landscape Project 2017) 'The Ain Sakhri Lovers' published in *Hwaet! 20 Years of Ledbury Poetry Festival* (Bloodaxe 2016). RUTH SHARMAN 'Eve Speaks' and 'Parable of the Sower' *Scarlet Tiger* (Templar Poetry 2016). PAT SIMMONS 'Fair Isle Fugue' was on display at St George's Concert Hall, Bristol as part of an exploration of the links between music and poetry. JANET SUTHERLAND 'Dusk' previously published as 'Blue Abrasions' *Hangman's Acre* (Shearsman Books 2009). SUSAN UTTING 'The Artist's Model Daydreams' *Striptease* (Smith/Doorstop Books.2001). 'Blonde' previously published as 'Warhol Blonde' in *Fair's Fair* (Two Rivers Press 2012). FIONA RITCHIE WALKER 'The Art of Folding' published in *Mslexia*. 'Inheritance' published in the *Carte Blanche* writing group anthology 2017. JOSIE WALSH 'Arrangement in Grey and Black No 1' and 'Body of Work' both in earlier versions *Breathing Space* (Ox-Eye Press 2004). JEAN WATKINS 'Interlocked' previously published as 'The Embrace' and 'Library' *Scrimshaw* (Two Rivers Press 2013). SUSAN WICKS 'Into Silence' and 'Capelle Catherinae, Visby Cathedral' *House of Tongues* (Bloodaxe 2011); 'Again' and 'This Art' *The Months* (Bloodaxe 2016). MERRYN WILLIAMS 'Admiring the Still Lives' *The First Wife's Tale* (Shoestring 2007). JACKIE WILLS 'Theatre' *Commandments* (Arc, 2007); 'A Bowl of Rice' commissioned by The Edible Construction Company for a 2007 exhibition at the Jubilee Library, Brighton.

Joy Howard is the founder of Grey Hen Press, which specialises in publishing the work of older women poets. Her poems have featured in many anthologies and journals and can be found online at *poetry p f.* She has edited sixteen previous Grey Hen Press anthologies, and published a collection of her own poems *Exit Moonshine* about her 'coming out' experiences in the 1980s. Her second collection, *Refurbishment*, was published by Ward Wood in 2011, and her most recent, *Foraging*, by Arachne Press in 2016.